Looking Up!

Finding My Voice in Las Vegas

He is an individual that young people should want to know.

— Bill Cosby, entertainer

William H. "Bob" Bailey was on the front lines of the civil rights movement in southern Nevada and instrumental in opening the hotel and gaming industry to minorities by providing training in jobs traditionally reserved for the white citizens. Bob's success is grounded in his belief that education and training are the keys to success for every American.

— Harry Reid, Senate Majority Leader
United States Senate

His accomplishments in bringing needed social change to Nevada are noteworthy. Mr. Bailey is an advocate of education as a means to societal responsibility.

— John Ensign, United States Senator

Dr. William "Bob" Bailey's leadership and great ability to achieve in difficult circumstances has set him apart from others and is truly an indication of the positive role model he is to any youth.

— Kenny C. Guinn, former Nevada governor

Dr. Bailey has been a true champion of educational excellence for all children. His diverse, tireless involvement in and support of civic, community, and educational services has been absolutely exemplary.

— Yolanda McKinney-Arrington, Director
Academic Support, Educational Accountability, and Government Relations, Clark County School District, Las Vegas, Nevada

Mr. Bailey possesses a keen analytical mind that is able to go directly to the heart of a problem and find a solution.

— Willard and Dianna Booth

His non-confrontational approach to a problem has served this community well and has brought us closer together.

— Burton M. Cohen

With the social grace, a calm intellectual approach, and a constant tenacious commitment, Bob Bailey accomplished in 25 short years, what looked impossible to accomplish in a hundred years.

— Ken Dab-Row, Dab-Row Broadcast Advertising

With his experience and accomplishments, he has made a tremendous impact on the state of Nevada as it relates to education, jobs, equal rights, social change, and economic development.

— Pastor Willie Davis, Second Baptist Church

I know Dr. Bailey to be honest, caring, and diligent in serving to make a difference. He is a devoted family man and in all ways a fine role model for our children and our community.

— Norma de la Cerna

Mr. Bailey instilled in me and many other wayward students that getting an education was attainable for anyone who worked hard. He also encouraged us not to be detained by trials and tribulations. He is a man of rectitude, probity, integrity, character, and commitment.

— Ernest M. Fountain, New Venture Capitol Development Company

I have the highest respect and regard for Dr. Bailey, his family, his work ethic, and the good he has done and continues to do in this community.

— Joseph P. Delaney, columnist, *Las Vegas Sun*

William Bob Bailey has given so much to others as a leader and role model.

— Michael L. Douglas, District Judge
Nevada Supreme Court

William H. "Bob" Bailey worked unselfishly and tirelessly to integrate blacks into mainstream society. He worked strenuously to improve their living conditions. He fought to integrate Las Vegas hotels, casinos, restaurants, and businesses and fought for school integration.

— Lee A. Gates, District Judge, Eighth Judicial District
Court, Las Vegas, Nevada

Dr. William "Bob" Bailey is a pillar of the community and respected by all in the community.

— Chic Hecht, former U.S. Ambassador

It would do the community proud to have a school named in his honor.

DeeDee Jasmin, Educating Through The Arts, Founder

From his early days at the Moulin Rouge to his leadership in the African American community, Bob is certainly the kind of role model our children need.

— Kara J. Kelley, Las Vegas Chamber of Commerce
President and CEO

As one in the forefront of the Civil Rights movement and its quest for social change in America, Dr. Bailey was adamant and outspoken about the need for education and training to take advantage of equal opportunity when the barriers of discrimination and segregation of African-Americans were torn down.

— Alice Key

The name Bob Bailey is synonymous with terms such as, diversification, parity, equality, inclusion, knowledge, hard work, and fairness. We have the highest respect and admiration for his dedication, commitment, and inclusion of all people in his mission to make our city and country a better place to live.

— Horacio Lopez, President
Southern Nevada Courier Service, Inc.
— George Lopez, President
Amalgamated Safety Company

Bob brought great honor to Las Vegas and Nevada and he shines as a bright star to all young black children. Every child sees in Bob that success is only limited by dedication. If you work hard, serve your community and mankind, you will succeed.

— Ann T. Lynch, VP Community Services
Sunrise Hospital & Medical Center

His knowledge of the educational needs of the students in Las Vegas is recognized by his endeavors promoting scholarships for deserving prospects. To remedy some of the social and educational needs of many of the children in Las Vegas it is recommended that the personality of Dr. Bailey could be a catalyst for educational growth and an inspiration to them.

— Walter Mason

He has successfully nurtured several business enterprises and groomed numerous individuals including myself for solid career advancement. He has led an exemplary life dedicated to excellence, leadership, and high achievement.

— Rose McKinney-James, President
Brown & Partners

I witness his work as an individual who not only has championed change, but has been effective in helping to bring about those changes that have been beneficial to this state. Mr. Bailey's life in Nevada has been characterized by the kind of constructive activism and practical accomplishments that would be inspirational to the youth of this community.

— Dr. Paul E. Meacham, UNLV

I, for one, appreciate the trail that Bob has blazed for those in the African American community, and believe that all of Las Vegas and Nevada owes a debt to Bob.

— Dr. Anthony Pollard, President
Rainbow Medical Center

I always have been impressed by Dr. Bailey's contributions, most importantly, to his constant philosophical adherence to the admonition that "Education is the Key." Dr. Bailey never failed to keep reminding those of us who have worked with him that without proper training and education equal opportunity is meaningless.

— Sarann Knight Preddy

This was one specific project Dr. Bailey put his heart and soul into; one which made a significant difference in opening doors for minorities in the radio and TV broadcast industry.

— Sylvia Staples

Dr. Bailey's many years of contribution not only represent a career of the highest ethical standards, but also one of excellent leadership. We should honor him for his dedicated effort and for working so diligently to improve the quality of life for every citizen.

— Gary Reese, City of Las Vegas

A wonderful leader in the African American Community, Dr. Bailey is an asset to Clark County of immeasurable proportion. A self-made lifelong Nevadan, who is known for lending a helping hand to anyone that asks and who has brilliantly represented our community, our state, and our nation in all of his endeavors.

— Sig Rogich, President
The Rogich Communications Group

Bob is dedicated to the American dream and our young people through training and education.

— Allan D. Sachs, former President of
the Stardust Hotel

William H. "Bob" Bailey made it a mission to foster advancement through education. Bob has also made a considerable impact in the political arena in Clark County through the formation and leadership of the National Black Republican Round Table.

— Milton I. Schwartz

He has touched many lives and contributed greatly to human rights, education, arts and economic development. I know Dr. Bailey to be honest, caring and diligent in serving to make a difference in the lives of others. He is a devoted family man and in all ways a fine role model for our children and our community.

— Steve Sisolak, University and Community College System of Nevada Board of Regents

Bob Bailey is an outstanding citizen and has served his community with dignity and honesty. He is the model for citizenship and self-motivation. The children in this community have benefitted far beyond their knowledge from the contributions of Bob Bailey. Life in southern Nevada is far better today and will be tomorrow because of Bob Bailey.

— A. Allan Stipe, President and Chief Executive Officer Sunrise Hospital & Medical Center

Nevada should be proud to have a gentleman of his stature.

— Herb Tobman, Western Cab Company

Bob was a great leader and advocate opposed to bigotry and discrimination. He was also very courageous at a time in the early 1960s before the adoption of the 1964 federal civil rights law when he accepted hostility as a part of the job.

— Daniel R. Walsh, Law Offices of Walsh & Walsh

A positive role model for our young people, an excellent example proving that hard work and determination are the pathways to success.

— Shelley Berkley, United States Congresswoman

With passion, Mr. Bailey encouraged students with surmountable odds that an education was attainable for anyone who worked hard. He was instrumental in many students, including myself, continuing and pursuing their education. Our students need positive role models that have integrity, morals, and last but not least, character. Mr. Bailey is a man with all those facets. Mr. Bailey's philosophy "Reach One – Teach One" is so appropriate for his promise to the students in Nevada.

— Marcia L. Washington, Nevada State Board of Education, Nevada State Board for Occupational Education

Dr. Bailey has continuously worked to promote economic empowerment in the community. He was instrumental in the formation of the Latin and Black Chambers of Commerce as well as the Nevada Minority Business Council, and has remained an outspoken advocate for minority and small businesses for over forty years.

— Lawrence Weekly, Commissioner, City of Las Vegas

He is a strong and positive community figure that truly cares about education and self-advancement in today's youth. He cares enough to make a difference in the community by economic means and values education.

— John H. Wesley, CEO, Wesley Corporation

Most inspiring is Bob's devotion to his family. Bob's children are a reflection of the loving, supporting environment they grew up in and are following in his footsteps and fulfilling their dreams.

— Mary Louise Williams

Dr. William "Bob" Bailey helped shape the Nevada we know today. He is a pioneer in the truest sense of the word, having championed civil rights and human rights for all Nevadans. He is a role model, whose life is a blueprint for others to emulate.

— Monroe and Brenda J. Williams

Bob's success in breaking racial barriers in education, business and government, establishing educational and job training programs, and providing leadership of the Frederick Douglas Scholarship Fund is testimony to his commitment to serving his community.

— Claudine Williams

He has been admired and applauded for being a well-informed civic leader, active on the local, state, and national level. Many looked to Bob when leadership qualities were required. His wide range of abilities throughout the years is a source of pride for the African American community, as well as the Las Vegas community as a whole.

— Bruce L. Woodbury

Proud as he is of civil rights laws he helped pass, Bailey believes that today learning the ropes of business, the professions, and technology will do the most to improve the lives of minorities.

— A.D. Hopkins, *The First 100*

. . . promote lifeolong learning to students who will achieve and significantly contribute to our society as creative, ethical, problem solving citizens.

— Dedication, May 3, 2006
William H. "Bob" Bailey Middle School

Looking Up!

Finding My Voice in Las Vegas

Dr. William H. "Bob" Bailey

Stephens Press ❦ Las Vegas, Nevada

Certain passages of this book are drawn from interviews with Bob and Anna Bailey condicted for the Oral History Research Center at the University of Nevada–Las Vegas. The publisher and editors wish to thank the center and its director, Claytee White, for her assistance.

Editors: Mike and Joan Weatherford
Copy Editor: Jami Carpenter
Designer: Sue Campbell
Publishing Coordinator: Stacey Fott

Cataloging in Publication Data
Bailey, William H.
Looking up : finding my voice in Las Vegas / William H. Bailey.
240 p. : photos ; 23 cm.

ISBN: 1-935043-04-8
ISBN-13: 978-1-935043-04-1

Dr. William H. "Bob" Bailey relates the story of his life from his youth in Cleveland to his days as an entertainer and then as a businessman and civil rights advocate in Las Vegas, Nevada.

1. Bailey, William H., 1927- 2. African Americans—Nevada—Las Vegas—Biography. 3. Civil rights movements—Nevada—Las Vegas. 4. Las Vegas (Nev.)—History. I. Title.

[92] dc22 2009 2008944098

Post Office Box 1600
Las Vegas, NV 89125-1600
www.stephenspress.com

Printed in United States of America

*To Anna for over a half century of love,
devotion, compassion, and understanding.
To my son and daughter, John and
Kimberly, their spouses Teri and Charles, my
grandchildren, Jonathan, Jordan, Gabrielle,
Ali, and Brandon.*

*To my father, John, my mother, Margaret,
and my sister Francine in memories for the
love, confidence, and inspiration they gave to
me which has lasted for a lifetime.*

Contents

Foreword

I have a dream that my four little children will one day live in a nation where they will not be judged by the color of their skin, but by the content of their character.

— Martin Luther King Jr., August 28, 1963

Every year, people of every nationality, race, and religion, come to Las Vegas to enjoy the fine dining, fabulous entertainment, and world class resorts. But Las Vegas was not always open to everyone, and without the tireless efforts of William "Bob" Bailey, the injustices and inequalities prevalent then would have persisted even longer.

When Bob Bailey first came to Nevada in the 1950s, segregation was commonplace. Blacks and whites wined, dined, and lived separately; even Strip headliners couldn't stay at the hotels where they performed if they were African American.

In the late 1960s and early '70s, while I was tackling civil unrest and discrimination in schools as superintendent of the Clark County School District (which included the city of Las Vegas), Bob had already been battling for equal rights and desegregation in the community at large.

His dedication and perseverance were instrumental in the passage of major equal rights legislation, the development of affirmative action programs, and the creation of economic opportunities for all. His commitment to equal educational opportunities helped establish funding for scholarships and tutoring programs for minority students.

He could have lived quietly in Las Vegas, enjoying the dividends of a successful musical career. Instead, he put his reputation on the line and used his celebrity status to bring politicians, power brokers, and the black community together to resolve issues of inequality and racial discrimination. His hope for an integrated society kept him busy thinking of new programs and business opportunities as well as serving on the boards of various organizations and agencies dedicated to a better society.

Bob Bailey has continued to stand up for others and right the wrongs of previous generations, paving the way for future generations to experience equality in all avenues. Through sheer determination, Bailey broke through the barriers of discrimination, becoming a role model for what he did as much as for what he believed. His memoir is a testament to a life of public service.

It is an honor and a privilege to call William Bailey a fellow Nevadan and my friend for over forty years.

—Kenny Guinn, Nevada Governor 1999–2007

Special Thanks

To my nephews and nieces and the many family friends who have provided guidance and support to my personal as well as my professional life. Mentors who advised and assisted in the phases of my career, starting with John Hammond and Count Basie, as well as Clarence Robinson in my varied show business career. They built on a solid foundation that I had from my mentor at Morehouse, Dr. Benjamin Mayes. My previous mentor in Las Vegas, Dr. West; Andy Bruner, Governor Grant Sawyer, Burton Cohen. For the tenure of my minority business development involvement, I was fortunate to have the mentorship of Cleveland Neal; and Louis Barnet, a friend and brilliant colleague. The loyal and faithful chairman of NEDCO for 19 years, colleague Reverend Marion Bennett.

An extra special thanks to Vera Matthews who waded through my handwritten notes to type the manuscript for this book.

And lastly, to my many friends and associates whose names do not appear in this book, please accept my heartfelt thanks for your contributions to my life.

Introduction

PARTS OF MY LIFE HAVE BEEN EXTRAORDINARY; other experiences have been sadly common, at least for a black American of my generation. Perhaps it's those moments when the two collided that have defined me and will convince you to come along as I share my story.

I HAVE BEEN DRIVING ALL NIGHT, BUT I'M NOT as tired as I should be. The excitement of seeing my wife and starting a new phase of our life keeps me going through the night on a drive from New York that was supposed to take two or three times this long. I pull onto Fremont Street, the famous "Glitter Gulch" with its neon facades promising instant riches inside, but it's not the avenue I'm seeking.

I see a police car and stop to ask for directions to "D" Street and Van Buren. The officer gives me and my 1955 Oldsmobile 98 the once-over, then answers a question with a question.

"You here for that colored show at the new hotel?" he grumbles.

I am. My wife and I have traveled this country as a singer and dancer, and we're excited to be part of an incredible show at a first-rate property — an integrated oasis called the Moulin Rouge. The officer gives me directions that lead across some railroad tracks, under a bridge and to the Westside, the section of town dedicated to the minority community. My big fancy car veers off the paved streets and onto dirt roads, threading through patches of tumble-down shacks and outhouses. Suddenly, New York City is very far away.

DOWNTOWN LAS VEGAS WAS NOT A FRIENDLY place for black people in the segregated Las Vegas of the 1950s. The Strip was blossoming into a glamour spot for the Hollywood crowd, thanks to upscale casinos such as the Sands and entertainers the likes of Frank Sinatra. That left Fremont Street, the original Strip of the World War II era, to a different set of tourists: the "rednecks" and "shit-kickers."

So here I am, almost a year after my first glimpse of Glitter Gulch, walking through the front door of the Fremont Hotel. A security guard stops me to announce I'm not welcome. I already know that, so I beat him to the punch and ask for directions to the TV station on the second floor. He not only directs me, he follows to make sure I don't get lost. I walk toward the elevator. He suggests taking the stairs.

I make it to the studios of KTNV, Channel 13, and meet with the station manager. I had been given a great offer to become a TV personality for the station on the coattails of hosting a late-night variety show on Channel 8 while working at the Moulin Rouge.

I sign the agreement, then go down the stairs and start to walk out of the hotel. The same security guard follows me from the bottom of the steps to — and out — the front door. This goes on for about two weeks, until one day the station manager calls me into his office. It seems my traffic patterns have come to the attention of the hotel manager, who has requested I start using the back employees' entrance.

'I may not walk through that front door,' I tell myself, 'but the young brothers and sisters of Las Vegas will see someone on TV who looks like them.' A picture really is worth a thousand words.

It's a few years later and I'm in the lobby of a different hotel in another town. The El Capitan is really the only game around when it comes to lodging in Hawthorne, Nevada. In fact, it accounts for about half the economy, along with the U.S. Navy Ammunition Depot.

My two white colleagues are filling out their hotel registrations when one of them asks the desk clerk about the lack of attention toward me. "The El Capitan does not accommodate colored people," the clerk responds.

That's more than a little ironic. I'm only here because of chairing Nevada's Equal Rights Commission; the only minority member of a five-person committee charged with gathering evidence of racial discrimination around the state. I sure didn't have to look very far today.

The governor's office made the room reservations, but this desk clerk isn't having any of it. By now a crowd is gathering. I look to see if anybody has a white hood in his hands.

The manager comes out. My colleagues explain I'm chairman of a state commission, acting at the will of the governor and legislature. But the manager supports his clerk. It's the house policy, he says, and he can't make an exception unless the owners tell him different. One of my fellow commissioners opts to stay. The others come with me. We drive around until we are finally accepted at a motel on the outskirts of town.

The next morning we're scheduled to have hearings in Hawthorne to gather testimony about discriminatory policies around town. I get up bright and early. It promises to be an interesting day.

WHEN I LOOK BACK AT MY LIFE, IT FEELS LIKE A dream, or maybe a stage play I had a part in. Truthfully, I don't think I would have started this long journey of writing a biography, of remembering, if I hadn't been honored as a namesake for a Las Vegas public school, the Dr. William H. "Bob" Bailey Middle School. During the nomination process, letters of recommendation from those familiar with my work and community service throughout the years reminded me of my commitment to education and the unwavering, constant belief that "education is the light that blinds ignorance." It is my hope the school will stand as a monument to this conviction.

This book was certainly not written as an epic or drama, or intended to be a guide to a successful life. It is simply one black man sharing his experiences in this country during an incredible time in its history. I have seen technology take the car from a luxury to a necessity, witnessed the birth of television, the computer age, organ transplants, and space exploration. Most vividly, I have witnessed our "separate but equal" schools go through the painful but necessary experiment of integration, and watched the civil revolution that was brought about because a woman of color was not supposed to sit at the front of the bus. Citizens marched in the street, threatened by dogs and tear gas in order to make the guarantees of the United States Constitution available to all.

This personal history is also a look at the Las Vegas I remember and its evolution since 1955. There were times it was difficult to be here, particularly in those early days when this fledgling entertainment capital of the world, so liberated in some ways, was tethered by practices of racial segregation. Many of us muttered its reputation "Mississippi of the West" bitterly under our breaths. But I had always been interested in becoming a part of making things better and understood, thanks to the mentors in my life, that we all owe something to our community. I knew Las Vegas was a place to fulfill that commitment, that need to make things right. Every problem is an opportunity in the making.

As you read this book, I hope you will be able to transport yourself, and get the full impact of my emotions and excitement at the various stages of my life, from singer, to TV personality, to businessman, to equal-rights advocate.

You may agree with some of the things I did and disagree with others; you may come up with solutions I didn't see at the time. But remember, you are living in a time when the social and economic conditions are very different. White or black, you are basking under the shade of trees whose seeds were planted long ago.

Finally, there have been many people who have helped me understand myself during this lifetime, taught me how important it is to have goals and principles, and I am grateful to them. I must say that fate has also played a significant role. There were times when opportunities seemed to simply tap me on the shoulder. The lyrics were there, so to speak; it was up to me to make the music. My continued faith is also reborn nearly every day as I meet people from all walks of life who are willing to give of themselves for the benefit of others. I now approach the sunset of my life hoping to continue to provide a value to the existence God has so graciously granted me, for there is no greater purpose, no greater necessity.

Chapter 1

Growing up in America

"I'm the iceman baby, I sell the coldest stuff in town. . . ."

THE ICEBOX WAS THE FORERUNNER OF THE refrigerator, and it took anywhere from twenty-five to one hundred pounds of ice to keep it cold. Someone had to bring the ice. For a short period of time, that's exactly what I did in my hometown of Cleveland, Ohio. And I was good at it — for age sixteen, anyway.

To do the job, I got up at 4 AM and made it to the icehouse by 5:30 AM With an ice pick and pair of tongs in hand, I would load eight 100-pound blocks into the truck. The blocks had creases running down their sides so I could sever them as needed into chunks of twenty-five pounds. Then I would drive up and down the streets, looking for the signs people displayed in their windows if they needed a restock.

I wore a rubberized scarf over my shoulders so I could carry a block without it slipping off into the dirt. This was great, until the ice started melting and the freezing water started to run down my back and into my trousers. When I only had to go to the first floor it didn't demand much effort. But as I delivered to the second and third floor, it got harder to get up those stairs — kind of like life, I guess.

One flight, two flights, over and over. My soggy clothes and shoes would start to squish by the end of the route, and even at sixteen my arms and legs would ache. Some icemen wouldn't even respond to the window signs if they were on the third floor. Sales at that level were beyond their scope. But I was always determined to make another sale. I didn't mind going that extra mile, climbing those flights of stairs with my block of ice.

I WAS BORN IN DETROIT ON VALENTINE'S DAY, 1927, just in time to spend my childhood in the Great Depression. I grew up with my sister, Francine, who was ten years older than I. My mother had given birth to four children, but one sister died before I was born and another had infantile paralysis, passing away when I was an infant.

My father, John, lost his job with Ford Motor Company during those early years, but he found work in the stable of a Cleveland dairy thanks to a cousin who was the foreman. This was still the era of horse-driven milk wagons, so the horses had to be brushed, bedded-down and fed. This was Dad's job and he did it well. He wasn't making a lot of money, but we never wanted for milk, butter, or ice cream.

Family members later told me I was so mischievous — some would say plain "bad" — as a three-year-old, friends would fake not being at home by pulling their shades down when they saw my mother bringing me along for a visit. I would do things like reach into our goldfish bowl and pull out the fish to play with, turn the family pictures around to face the wall, or step on the cat's tail. Mother used to thank God she hadn't killed me by the time I was seven, when I finally became a productive member of the family.

My mother, Margaret, didn't do the day labor that smart "colored" women were driven to do. Though she wanted to bring in needed extra money, my father would not allow it. He wanted her to keep the home and be with the children. But in those days families worked together to provide the money needed for necessities and an occasional luxury, like a movie or a floor-style radio. So Dad took extra part-time work, my sister helped out by getting a weekend job and I, beginning at age seven, used my recently-acquired red wagon to help people carry their groceries home from the corner A&P store.

This was the beginning of my entrepreneurial journey. I became known as "the boy with the red wagon." I only worked 93rd Street, and in most cases I didn't have to cross the roadways. Even when I did, there was little traffic because so few of my neighbors had automobiles; yes, they were still called "automobiles" back in the early 1930s. My business went so well, the manager of the grocery store gave me a little tip on Saturday evenings for accommodating his customers. I was also earning my place in the household. At the dinner table I was a little man; I could "speak without being spoken to."

But as you grow, your responsibilities increase. Dad worked out a deal with the landlord to be the janitor for the twelve-unit apartment complex. I hated to see winter approach because that meant snow. Oh, did it snow in Cleveland. If there were two things I hated to do, it was shovel snow and pitch coal into the boilers at the apartment building. But with Dad having to work two jobs, I was elected to do both.

Shoveling snow wasn't so bad, but it was an everyday annoyance. When you weren't working the new snow, you were shoveling the salted slush to prevent ice from building up. After you finished the snow scene, it was onward and upward — or rather downward — to the boiler room to feed the hungry furnaces. The doors to the boilers resembled yawning mouths waiting to be fed, and I was the anointed feeder. Shovel after shovel, I would keep going until their bellies were full. Then it would be time for homework. What a day.

It was tough, but when Dad looked me in the eyes and said how much he appreciated my help, I was ready to do it all over again. He was always a role model for me, a self-taught man who was not only a hard worker, but decent, compassionate, with a love of family. He was just a good person.

We eventually moved out of the apartments with the beasts in the basement. In fact, I credit Franklin Delano Roosevelt for rescuing me from those hungry furnaces. In 1935, his Federal Housing Administration started building a dozen public-housing projects throughout the country and we moved into Outhwaite Homes at East 55th Street and Woodland Avenue, a safe, decent housing complex. Not only did we have a modern hot-water heater and stove, we even had a plot of ground to plant a victory garden.

I entered my teens tall and thin, with a fair set of good looks. I was doing well at Kennard Junior High School, just a short walk from our new home, and had a good weekend job at a meat market. My responsibilities were to scrape the cutting blocks clean, rotate the meat in the freezer and make sure the sawdust on the floor was fresh. Mom was finally letting me have an allowance to befit a hard-working teenager. After all, a fellow had to stop by the soda fountain and flirt with the girls. This action always required having nickels to drop in the jukebox.

The projects, at that time, were considered hot stuff. I know you had to meet some high standards of credit and character to be considered for one of the units. If you made it, you had access to a job developer who helped find work for the men, and after-school and summer jobs for the youth. Outhwaite also had an outdoor ice rink and a recreation center offering a number of youth and senior activities including Boy and Girl Scouts, baseball and basketball. Two of the friends I played with in the projects were Carl and Louis Stokes. Carl went on to become the first black mayor of Cleveland in 1967 — in fact the first African American to hold that position in any major U.S. city — and his brother, Louis, became a U.S. Congressman.

But the activity that would eventually change it all for me was singing in the Outhwaite glee club. We sang spirituals, folk songs and a few classics with singers ages fifteen to fifty. From lyric tenors to mature bass voices, we had it all. We were so popular that invitations to sing in the various all-city holiday events were always coming our way. The director gave me my first experience with public speaking when he started calling on me to introduce the choir. I would have to tell the crowds about our background and, of course, impart how glad we were to be invited. Maybe he noticed me running my mouth. I don't know. Regardless, this early confidence-builder would only help my early efforts to become a wooer, once I realized there were girls out there waiting to be wooed.

I looked about three years older than my real age of fifteen, and I thought I was a hot shot. But that didn't last. I had no idea how to talk to girls. 'But who could resist a suave singer?' I thought to myself. Some of my friends were thinking the same thing. Four of us were broken off into a quartet for the glee club, and after rehearsals we would stand on the street corner, under the street light, and sing what our director called "low class, flash-in-the-pan" music. But we couldn't get enough of this "low-class" stuff, songs like: "You Made Me Love You," "Stardust," and "There'll Be Some Changes Made." It's funny, the director probably felt the same way my generation feels about rap today.

As luck would have it, we were noticed at our impromptu shows and started getting invitations to sing at parties. We liked this because, of course, it gave us a chance to meet some girls and finally do some pursuing.

After six months of singing at parties and around town, we decided to form an official group. The best name we could come up with was, The Four Notes. But we sounded good, patterning ourselves after the Ink Spots, who had their first big hit in 1939 with "If I Didn't Care," and would dominate radio during the World War II years with hits such as "We Three." Our voices matched theirs so it was easy to copy that style. I was the first tenor, Tracy Crittenden was the second, William "Bubble" Carpenter was the baritone and Ed "Spits" Cunningham the bass. We took off like a rocket. We could sing like the Mills Brothers, who already had been going strong since the early 1930s, for the older folks, spirituals from the Blind Boys of Alabama for the church crowds, and music of the day by the Ink Spots for the teen parties.

One day, after about a year of performing, one of us finally asked, "Why aren't we making any money doing this?" By now I had hassled my parents to subsidize my wardrobe needs of a jacket, shirt, and tie to match (red, of course). I was the youngest of the four, and while Bubble and I were still in high school, Tracy and Spits had already graduated and were working their first full-time jobs. Our only source of income as a singing group was from church performances because the members would take a collection for us. All other appearances were free. We started talking, and suddenly it dawned on one of us:

"Do you think maybe one of the reasons we're invited to perform so much is because our price is right?"

"You mean, free?"

It was time to get a business manager, and we did. I can't remember his name now, and we didn't keep him on very long after he took all the money from our first job. He did get us on the right track, though. As soon as we performed for money that first time, we were considered professionals. We had won a couple of school and church amateur hours, but there was one we hadn't been in: Major Bowes Amateur Hour. It was radio's best-known talent show, and you had to win two or three preliminary shows in your hometown to make the big one. If you did, you got to go on the radio for a weekend matinee broadcast from your city; in our case, the RKO 105th Street Theatre.

Ironically, it was none other than the Ink Spots appearing as the theater's evening attraction that week, and we were excited to learn that one of the prizes for being on the show was getting to meet them. We made it to the finals and went on the air to sing their hit, "This Is Worth Fighting For." When the song was finished, we heard someone walk up behind us. The crowd started laughing and applauding. I turned around to see the Ink Spots' six-foot-four front man, Bill Kenny, who towered over us.

"You have a lot of nerve singing that song that I made famous," he told us as the crowd roared. "But I forgive you because you did such a good job."

The Four Notes won the final contest and the whole black community was alive with pride. Our professional career was about to be launched. The invitations poured in, but now we wanted to be paid, which slowed the offers down a bit. One of the nightclubs wanted us on a weekly basis, but Dad wouldn't allow that during the school week. There was another pesky little detail: I was under age and had to pad my 16 years with my height and a pencil-thin mustache. We worked Friday and Saturday nights, and sometimes a Sunday afternoon matinee. But show business was paying off on the personal front. My biggest concern was how to keep my two girlfriends from knowing about each other. After some "real world" practice, I was becoming a pretty good wooer after all.

As for the "day job," Dad was reminding me that my school attendance was suffering and this was not acceptable. It wasn't that I didn't enjoy school, just that the activities of the quartet were keeping me up late and it was hard to wake up when the alarm clock went off at 5:30 AM. In those days, you walked to school if you didn't have the money to get a school pass for the streetcar. Besides, from Outhwaite you couldn't really get a direct streetcar to the school. You had to transfer twice, so it was easier just to walk. Sure, it was four miles. But you had the companionship of your friends. We talked about sex, music appreciation, sports, sometimes even class assignments. But mostly sex.

Cleveland had integrated schools back when the "separate but equal" doctrine was the rule. Though the majority of the students were black, there were whites and some Asians in the school. We had drama and music together, not recognizing our ethnic differences or color.

At age sixteen, I was already in my senior year. I can't remember if I skipped some grades along the way, or if my parents started me in school early. But I was pretty full of it for my age, probably because of the quartet. I was God's gift to the world. But one day I had a wake-up call. My homeroom teacher sat me down and told me, "If you don't start doing better in geometry class, you might not graduate." It was time to get serious: no more skipping classes, no more sleeping through history class, no more roaming in the hallways.

Still, my "fame" as the quartet's lead singer made me popular enough at school for my friends to convince me I should run for class president. I wondered if I could handle the workload on top of everything else, but decided to accept the challenge. My school buddy, Mary Louise Randolph, offered to help me with both my school work and the campaign. In the end, I won the election. I figured one fringe benefit of holding this high and exalted office might be that it would insulate me from academic failure. But then I was called to the principal's office.

In a firm voice, he told me I was expected to maintain at least a 3.5 grade point average, and provide behavioral leadership. And oh, by the way, there would be no special favors just because I was president. I decided maybe it was time to resign. Just then, my homeroom teacher interrupted.

"I think these are achievable goals for Bill. He's always displayed leadership qualities in the classroom."

The principal nodded and my teacher ushered me out of the office, thanking the principal for his concern and direction. My teacher reassured me that I'd get any help I needed to meet the academic requirements for graduation.

My singing was keeping me up late and interfering with school work, but, ironically, it was what got me into college. I was on the track team, but not considered an athlete on par with the football or basketball boys. I worked as a cheerleader, but having a megaphone on your athletic letter was not exactly macho. It became abundantly clear that my real strengths, and my aptitude, lie in drama, music, and English. Fortunately, the school system in Cleveland produced a good finished product and prepared us for college. And for high school seniors in 1943, it was a potentially life-changing policy that college students were exempt from the draft. A great number of my fellow students looked forward to attendance at "Negro colleges." Most of our role models had attended colleges in the South, which were developed to give black applicants an alternative-offering to the country's white-dominated schools. Many went on to "white" universities for master and doctorate degrees. I was awarded a vocal music scholarship to attend Morehouse College, the private, all-male school in Atlanta. Morehouse is the Harvard of the black schools, though later, as students, we would say, "Harvard is the Morehouse of the white schools."

Graduation drew near and I lined up my first-choice girl as a date for the senior prom. I broke into the piggy bank to share the cost of a limousine with a buddy of mine, and purchased a corsage, a box of candy, and a pint of the cheapest wine I could afford for the party afterwards. But on the morning of the prom, the roof caved in. It turned out my date had a boyfriend in the armed services, and he decided to come home to see her before going overseas. I was blown out of the water! Suddenly, my date was his date. Should I give him my limo ride, the corsage, the box of candy? Hell no.

I needed to regroup and think of something. I called my aggressive girlfriend, but she had pigeonholed one of the football players. Not a very bright guy, but he looked good in a tux. I was in luck with my next call. I had a friend who was pretty but, how do I put this? Kind of a nerd, and known to be a virgin. But the most important thing on this day was that she had not been asked by anyone. In fact, her father had volunteered to act as her escort. As a result of my invitation, her father was so happy to get off the hook that he offered to pay for the limo and give me the credit at the florist for a corsage. All in all, everything turned out great. She never mentioned schoolwork and even took two swigs of champagne. (Thanks to her dad's money, I upgraded from the cheap wine.) I never found out if she was a virgin, and nothing changed that night if she was, but we had fun.

Our graduation ceremony was heralded by the school band playing the National Anthem out of tune, sung by a pretty singer who couldn't sing on key. Some people in the audience applauded because they were happy that someone in their family made the cut. Others were just happy the music was finally over. After we received our diplomas, some of us talked about college and what summer jobs awaited us to help with our freshman college expenses. Others were facing the real world of work and its emerging responsibilities, while still others were preparing to go to war.

The war effort was in full swing in Cleveland and manual jobs were plentiful. People scrambled to get the good defense jobs in the assembly plants, which left a number of lower-paying ones open. My first job out of high school, acquired through a fellow classmate, was at a battery plant. The pay was good and no experience was required. The workday started at 7 AM, which meant you had to get up at 5 AM to get there on time. But that was OK; I was going to college.

I should have had more of a clue about a job description labeled "boiler attendant." My mind should have flashed back to the old boiler days, when I was helping Dad with the janitorial bit. But it didn't register. I was exalted over the fact I had a job that paid good money and started soon. The weekend before that first Monday of work had to be the longest of my sixteen-year-old life. Finally, the morning arrived and I reported to my assigned building. I met the foreman, and he showed me the boiler and the mountain of coal I had to shovel into the boiler-assembly chain. The foreman gave a friendly smile. "You get a fifteen-minute break every forty-five minutes," he assured me.

What a great job! With gusto, I pitched into the material with my shovel and almost went to the floor. It felt like I was lifting pure lead. Each load must have weighed at least forty to fifty pounds. The only way I finished that day was to keep thinking, 'this is why I'm going to college.' It was a body-buster. Each night, Mom had to rub me down with liniment so I could work the next day.

My foreman was very encouraging. He would pass by my station and ask me how I was doing.

"I'm hurting!"

"Don't worry. In a month or two, you'll feel like a new man."

If he would have said a week or two, I might have stayed the course. But the thought of the aches and pains for another two months was more than I could justify to my body. Not even the sure-fire motivator, 'This is why I'm going to college,' was working anymore. After two weeks and a good paycheck, I thanked the foreman, waved my arms and said, "I'm out of here."

After a brief rest period, I started searching for another job that would last as long as the summer. My uncle Willie said an Italian friend he drinks red wine with had just the job for me: good pay, no special expertise required and you meet interesting people. Perfect for an aggressive self-achiever. When I asked for the job title, he said, "Iceman."

So there I was the iceman, and if I sounded a little too noble at the beginning of the chapter — for that is the way chapters are supposed to begin — here is a story to temper that nobility.

It turns out the old blues song, "Coal and Iceman Blues," recorded by Sonny Boy Williamson and others, wasn't just bragging: "Anytime you get hot baby, call up your iceman and I'll cool you down." There were ladies on the route who were indeed willing to trade certain services in lieu of cash.

I wasn't a week into the job when I spotted a sign in a third-floor window for seventy-five pounds, a big order. I carted the ice upstairs and was met by a cute young woman closer to my sister's age, maybe in her early twenties. I went through the routine we usually did for older customers, widows, or those known to tip: trimmed down what little ice was still left in the icebox to accommodate the new piece, then emptied the water pan that caught the melted ice underneath. Finished with this ritual, I turned to her for my pay. With a curt smile and a caress of her hips, she advised me that she was short of cash but she would like to negotiate a deal. I was very excitable at that age, and what else was I going to do? Take all that ice back down the stairs?

I stayed in her apartment about two hours. It was my first such experience, my growing-up period. I glided down the stairs and out the door, only to be slapped in the face by the sight of half my load of ice gone, melted into a puddle of water under the truck and running into the sewer. It was an expensive lesson which cost me two-days pay to reimburse. When I told the older icemen what happened, they just howled. Some of them had the same experience when they first started the job, and some of them also had routes that included a little extra customer service for the widow women. Their advice: "You always save that for the end of the run." Make the "exchange sales" the last ones on the route, when most of your ice has already been sold and you don't have much left. I took that advice. Needless to say, my friend who lived by herself on the third floor became a regular customer that summer.

IT WAS FINALLY TIME FOR MY DEPARTURE. Mother put together a going-away party for me and just happened to mention, "If you bring a pair of socks or some underwear to the party with you, it would be well-appreciated." This was done without Dad's knowledge or he would have gotten on Mom's case. But when he saw them, he agreed the gifts were a nice gesture for the first Bailey in the family to go to college. The most touching going-away present was one my uncle Willie brought me: an envelope with ten dollars from the icemen. The card said, "Study hard and be somebody. See you next summer — your job will be waiting!"

The day I left there were wet eyes everywhere: my sister and her friends who had known me since I was a baby; my uncle, James, and his wife; two of the neighbors; Mom and Dad. You would think it was a wake instead of the launch for the greatest challenge of my life, but I knew they were tears of happiness, not despair. Everyone had last-minute instructions and I nodded my head in respect.

"Always keep your money in your shoe."

"Mind your elders."

"Go to church."

"Don't argue with white folks."

And above all, "Keep your ding in your pants."

Where else would I keep it?

Chapter 2

Morehouse and Life Down Home

On the day I left for Atlanta in 1943, I arrived at the train station with my family to find several friends already waiting for their own departures. We gathered together, more than a dozen of us, nervously shifting our feet, many of us fumbling with the shoe boxes our mothers had stuffed with the last home-cooked goodies we would see for a while.

Some of my friends were going to Morehouse, others had chosen West Virginia State or Wilberforce University in southern Ohio. So we passed the time by teasing one another about the virtues of each school based on academics and, of course, the percentage of pretty girls. The shoe boxes were also targets of some ribbing, although about four hours into the trip we turned the tables by making these same friends watch us eat until finally offering them remnants of our fried chicken and biscuits or macaroni and cheese.

The first leg of the trip was to Cincinnati. We had a great time talking to one another, now and then leaning back and letting the train's low rumble and gentle rocking lull us to sleep. It was a good distraction. It took my mind off the reality that I was starting on a new path and going to a place I had only heard stories about, many of them with little nuance: The South was both glorious and a place to tread very, very carefully.

When we arrived in Cincinnati I finally got my first bitter taste of this duality, or the idea that you were allowed to chase your dreams only by staying within certain narrow boundaries. My uncle had offered some practical advice before I left Cleveland: Avoid the coach located behind a train's engine because the cinders and soot tend to blow backward and into the passengers' faces. When we arrived in Cincinnati we found our new train. But before we could board, it became clear we were expected go to the coach behind the engine; the choice of where we were going to sit was never an option that was ours. This was my first real experience with blatant segregation.

It was going to be a long trip from Cincinnati to Atlanta, so we talked, played games, and settled down for our journey. We weren't allowed in the dining car so they sent up some baskets filled with sandwiches that we could purchase. To think we had questioned our parents' logic of burdening us with those shoeboxes of food at the station. They obviously knew much more than we did. I must say, though, the conductor seemed to show some understanding of our situation.

John, one of my classmates who had traveled to Birmingham, Alabama to see his grandparents before, began to tell us stories, and share some do's and don'ts as we crossed the Mason-Dixon line.

"Be careful of the rednecks," he concluded. "They're bad news! When you see the red neck, go in the other direction."

I half laughed at this, but I must say I did look at the conductor's red, sunburned neck and wondered if even a rule as seemingly arbitrary as John's would serve well on this new adventure in the South.

When we arrived in Atlanta it was a relief to see the smiling faces of the Morehouse men waiting at the station. I will never forget the feeling of warmth and brotherhood, not to mention the breakfast of sausage, grits, gravy and biscuits they treated us to that morning. Of course, we were still freshmen. It wasn't long before these brothers of ours started whittling down our egos with epithets like "scumbag" and some kicks in the pants. It was all part of our initiation, and the next year it would be our turn to bring down the incoming freshman a peg or two.

Academically, the school was a challenge compared to the work we were used to in high school. But with college-preparatory classes under our belts, most of us managed to make it through the first year. I must admit, we were pretty cocky in the beginning, checking out the backgrounds of our instructors before classes even started that first semester. But our attitudes quickly adjusted when we saw "PhD" behind almost all of the names. Many of them had obtained their doctorates in Europe at schools such as Oxford, La Sorbonne, Cambridge, or one of several universities in Canada. Our president, Dr. Benjamin Mays, held a doctorate from the University of Chicago in the School of Religion. In fact, there were more PhDs per student at Morehouse during that time than Harvard, Yale, or Princeton. And there was good reason for this. The Ivy League schools did not hire black instructors to teach their white students, no matter how illustrious their academic background. But they were glad to be at Morehouse and Morehouse was glad to have them.

Atlanta, in fact, had such a sophisticated black community that it created its own world. There were five colleges open to African Americans in the city — Morehouse, Spelman, Clark, Morris Brown, and Atlanta University — and an entire society became their offspring. The black community had its own banks, restaurants, hotels, drug stores, grocery stores and various retailers. There was even a daily newspaper covering African American issues from around the world.

I didn't realize, however, how much different things were beyond the black community. One Saturday I took some time off from my studies to go downtown and purchase a hat. It wasn't Cleveland, but the winters in Atlanta could still get cold and required a top coat, scarf, gloves, and hat to fight back the winds and chill. I found a local haberdashery and, lo and behold, there was the perfect bowler in the display window.

I went inside and waited as the sales staff ignored me and serviced the white customers one-by-one. Finally, I was approached and asked why I was in the store. "It's a haberdashery," I thought. "What else would I want but a hat?"

The salesman was short, and I remember looking down at him and pointing to the bowler in the window. He asked me what size I wore but I didn't know, so I just said, "Big." He left for a minute then came back with the hat I wanted, size large. I went to the mirror and tried it on, and instantly realized I had made a mistake. I was not a size-large-hat kind of guy. It was so big it nearly covered my face. I turned to the salesman.

"Maybe I should try a medium," I said.

"No, that's yours," the salesman said.

"What do you mean it's mine? It's too large. I need something smaller."

"No respectable white man is going to put a hat on after you've put it on your head."

"But it's too big. I can't use it."

"Well it's yours, and you are going to pay for it or you're going to jail."

This "who's on first" routine went on for a while. As our voices started to rise, the manager came over and tried to quiet us down. When he learned what the dispute was about, he simply proceeded to tell me how I could wrap newspaper over the inside band of the hat to keep it from blowing off. He assured me I would be arrested if I did not pay for the requested merchandise. In the meantime, the salesman had sent for the police.

When the officer walked in, he didn't say a word. At that point, I immediately paid for the hat and left. I later traded it for a skullcap from one of my classmates. It wasn't as fashionable as the derby, or "Bubba" hat as we used to call them, but it managed to keep my not-so-large head warm for the winter.

This experience confused me. The black community had many people of means and I knew they would not allow themselves to be embarrassed as I was on that day. But when I asked one of my Atlanta friends why I was treated like an outcast and inquired, "What about the doctors and professional people?" he explained that when affluent black Atlantans buy clothes, the department stores send trucks to their homes with the requested sizes and colors, the customers purchase what they want and send the rest back.

This was the lifestyle of the polarized South. Everyone knew their place and worked around their differences. There were successful blacks living in the same style as their white counterparts, but their neighborhoods were separate. Some of the stately African American homes reminded me of the mansions in Cleveland that were serviced by black workers. In fact, Atlanta was the first place I ever encountered an African American servant working in the home of another African American, white gloves, butler suits, the whole bit.

But the two paths of upper-class blacks and whites rarely crossed.

Later in those college years, I had an even scarier reminder. A Spelman student named Dorothy and I volunteered to go to the warehouse district of Atlanta to pick up some materials for parade decorations. When we went to get our order, three or four white warehousemen surrounded us, faces taut and jaws squared. My companion leaned into me and placed her arm under mine.

"Nigger, whatcha doin' with this white woman?" one demanded.

"What white woman?"

"Don't get smart with me, nigger."

I realized Dorothy was light-skinned enough to confuse them. I tried to explain, but they weren't having any of it.

"You know what happens to niggers who go around with white girls? We beat 'em and then hang 'em."

Dorothy chimed in, explaining she only had some white blood on her father's side, before the clerk who sold us the materials came over to break up the situation. He told the men we were from the colleges, then looked at us and, very wisely, told us to leave. We were in such a rush to take his advice, we left without the boxes we came for.

My reaction to the social realities of Atlanta was as full of contradictions as the city itself. On the one hand, I had experienced a segregation that could come down with the subtlety of a hammer, or seep in slowly like a fog or a murmur in the ear, distorting reality for its own twisted purposes. But I was also a young man and practical in many ways. I was watching and learning, fascinated by the two worlds and how blacks could prosper in a captured economy as well as whites in an open economy.

The colleges of Atlanta were feeding this economic success by producing new crops of black professionals every year. The social success would have to come later. At Morehouse they never let us forget the importance of getting an education so that someday we could work toward bringing equal rights and opportunities to all Americans. President Mays was notorious for always reminding his students of the importance of giving back to the community. The lessons I learned in Atlanta, from both school and the nuances of the city's segregation, would stay with me for the rest of my life.

I admit I didn't have much opportunity to reflect upon segregation at the time because of all the activities Atlanta offered, including church events, school affairs, concerts, nightclubs. Besides, I was young and still getting used to being away from home.

I remember being invited to the homes of off-campus students and Morehouse graduates during holiday breaks when I couldn't make it back to Cleveland. Most of the students were from the South, where a train ride home was quick and inexpensive, but Cleveland was a long distance away. Our dormitories stayed open for those with nowhere to go during the holidays, but that initial Christmas alone was the first one I had ever spent away from my family. When it came, I watched the sun come up through my dormitory window, and I cried.

THERE WAS A DRUG STORE IN ATLANTA CALLED Yates and Milton where students used to gather. Their soda fountain was the best in the world, but it was the girls who made me feel like a kid in a candy store. Cleveland had some pretty women but the South, well, I had never seen so many beautiful ladies of color — from ebony black to peach-fuzz white.

It was at Yates and Milton where I made my singing debut freshman year. Word had gotten out that I was a singer of some renown in Cleveland and would be joining the college glee club during the second semester. A group of upper classmen decided I should make my first appearance at the drug store so I agreed, knowing these older classmates would see it as a chance to deflate the ego of another lowly freshman. But I was ready.

The place was filled with beautiful girls and those wishful brothers waiting for me to fall on my face. I started out with "This Is Worth Fighting For" by the Ink Spots. It had a lot of vocal range and ended on a high C which brought the house down. Then I sang "For Sentimental Reasons" to the ladies. It must have worked because a young woman I had spotted at the drug store earlier that semester came up and congratulated me on my performance. I decided to strike while the iron was hot and ask her for a date. She hesitated, then said, "I'll think about it."

My roommate told me later she was the girlfriend of a student pilot at Tuskegee who was training for the 99th Pursuit Squadron. He had some brothers who were looking after her in his absence.

"I'd be happy to do my patriotic duty and help them take care of her," I told my friend, although I did wonder how big the brothers were.

But singing pop songs for kids at a soda fountain would have to take a backseat for a while. It was time to start fulfilling my music scholarship by singing with the Morehouse College Glee Club. Singing in groups was not new to me, but the club's musical selections were something altogether different than my days with the quartet in Cleveland. These were classical songs, some of them in foreign languages, and spirituals I had heard before — but never like this. The way the upper classmen blended their strong voices in such beautiful harmony was inspiring and I wondered, for the first time, how voices could have the range and tone of a well-played instrument. I can still hear the words of our musical director Kipper Harold who would tell us, "Your voices are instruments, and that's how you should use them."

We toured around the South and in eastern cities such as Washington, Philadelphia, and Pittsburgh, usually performing in local churches where we were graciously received. I loved to watch the audiences respond to our singing, so proud they were of these little black boys who could master different languages and choral techniques. But their faces really lit up when we started in on the familiar — spirituals such as "Little David, Play on Your Harp," "Joshua Fit the Battle of Jericho," and "His Eye on the Sparrow" — eventually sweeping them up in the emotion and truth of these deep-rooted hymns. I admit, there were times I felt the emotion myself.

To this day, the Morehouse College Glee Club travels around the world sharing the authentic African American interpretation of our spirituals and songs, and in the various languages of the host countries. It is a wonderful experience for any young man, and a chance to be part of history.

Little did I know that history was standing just a few feet away from me during all those practices and sundry performances with my Morehouse brothers. I shared the stage with a fellow student named Martin Luther King Jr., an Atlanta preacher's son whom we all felt would be exceptional at whatever he chose to do with his life, yet had no way of knowing we were singing next to one of the greatest individuals of the twentieth century.

He was smart, religiously inspired, and easy to be around. I didn't spend much time with him socially, for the off-campus Morehouse students usually hung out with one another and the same went for the on-campus crowd. But there were times, after various church events, when his family invited the glee club members to their house for breakfast and we would dive into the grits, biscuits, and sausage. I guess you could say we all sang together, prayed together, and broke bread together. No one ever imagined we were evangelizing with a man who would lead the Civil Rights Movement, have tremendous influence on the history of this country, and provide an image for change throughout the world. And in the South, at that particular time, it took a very unique individual to provide leadership and not end up in the graveyard. Martin was that exceptional individual who was ready to engage himself at the moment when leadership was demanded.

After my days at Morehouse, I saw Martin only once. It was in the mid 1960s when he was invited by the Las Vegas chapter of the NAACP to speak at the Sands Convention Center and the Second Baptist Church on Madison Avenue. I was part of the entourage that met him at the airport and we greeted one another as old friends. As his visit wore on, we talked about our days at Morehouse, the friends we had in common and, of course, the movement and how Las Vegas could become a visible player in the national struggle for civil rights.

But one of the things I remember most about his visit was the security. From the moment he got off the plane there was at least one sheriff's deputy by his side, and while I was impressed by the protection he was receiving on the part of the U.S. Department of Justice and local law enforcement, it did bring home the weight of this man's immense responsibility.

While Martin was perhaps more cognizant than your typical Morehouse student of society's failings and may have understood, even back then, that he had a larger purpose, my focus was much narrower: school work and social activities. After getting a handle on my grades I began to get into the swing of the city's nightlife, especially on the weekends. A great night out was going to a movie and then dinner at the Chicken Shack. If you were lucky, you might take a walk around campus and find a spot to smooch a little before curfew.

Spelman had the toughest curfew but it had the most girls. In fact, in my opinion, it had the greatest variety of ladies of any school in the South. Sometimes, when I had classes on the Spelman campus, I would go early and sit on a bench to watch the young women parade by: chocolate, vanilla, chocolate mocha, caramel, butter pecan, and licorice. Without a curfew, a fellow could spend a lot of time chasing his own special flavor.

Unfortunately, I had little in my pocket to spend on dates should I catch one of these beauties. My mother eventually stopped hosting house parties to raise money for my schooling and incidentals, which meant I was receiving only enough to pay for books and supplies. Besides, times were tough and I knew my family needed the money to keep house and home together.

So, I took inventory of my talents, and tried to decide which ones I could use to create some income and still not interfere with my school schedule. As I reviewed my skills, I didn't come up with how much a young Morehouse student could market — except my singing. I would get a gig.

It was the mid 1940s, and the attitude back then in the midst of World War II was to live it up, especially among those brothers who were eligible for the draft. There were three prominent nightclubs in the black area of town. Two of those clubs catered to an older crowd, while the third attracted college students and young professionals. My roommate, Eddie Hall, agreed to be my manager and we decided the third club was the best fit for me. It was an intimate room with a capacity of about one hundred and a handful of tables in front of the stage. We approached the owner and I was hired to sing on the weekends. The pay wasn't much but as word of mouth spread, the crowds started growing and my boss agreed to give me a raise.

Life was good. My school work was going well, I was what you would call an overnight success at the club, and my spiritual life and social life were better than ever. As far as I was concerned, nothing could enter my world to top where I was at that moment in time. I was wrong.

On Thanksgiving eve of my third year, rain was coming down outside and there was an early-winter chill, but you could warm your hands by the atmosphere inside the club. Students from around Atlanta were on holiday break, and it seemed like half of them were inside the club laughing, talking loud, flirting with each other. It was all I could do not to pull up a chair and join the celebration, but despite my own relief at having a break from studies for a few days, it wasn't time to relax quite yet. I walked onto the stage to start one of my sets and looked out onto the crowd, smiling at the sea of animated, young black faces, when I noticed two older gentlemen sitting near the center of the room. They were white, but it wasn't the color of their skin that attracted my interest. This was what you would call a black-and-tan club. We were always getting white customers from surrounding schools such as Georgia Tech. But these were older, refined gentlemen, not loud or obnoxious, clearly responding to the music, whether it be blues or jazz. One of them also looked familiar but I didn't know why.

They caught two sets before the owner walked up and said they wanted to talk to me. My first thought was that they were gay, because I'd been approached by gay white customers before. If that was the case, I wasn't interested.

"Do they seem gay?" I asked.

"No, no. One of them said he's Benny Goodman."

I had seen Goodman at the Palace Theater in Cleveland. Now it all made sense, why he looked so familiar. Suddenly, I got very nervous. As I later learned, the second man was John Hammond, the renowned journalist and record producer, who enjoyed working as a conduit between the club-level entertainers and the record labels. He had helped Goodman organize his band, discovered a teenaged Billie Holiday and brought Count Basie from Kansas City to New York, setting up Basie's first recording deal just because he liked the band, with no money in it for him.

I floated over to their table in a rush of nerves and excitement.

"I'm John Hammond and this is my running mate Benny Goodman," Hammond said.

There was some chitchat about music, then out of the clear blue sky, they asked me if I'd like to sing with Count Basie.

"Oh, you're drunk," I said. "I would love to sing with Count Basie. How much does it pay?"

We all laughed and they said, "Enough."

It seems they were on a talent search and for some reason this small college hangout in Atlanta was on their radar. I kept thinking they were pulling my leg but as the conversation wore on, they asked if I'd be interested in flying out to New York for an audition with Basie. I said yes, and gave them the phone number for my dormitory. A week went by, then two. I was starting to think they had forgotten or the whole thing was a hoax. Finally, two days before I was to go home for Christmas vacation, someone yelled down the hallway from the communal phone: "Bailey! New York calling!" My heart skipped as I ran, then tried to regain composure to talk to John Hammond.

"When is your Christmas vacation?" he asked. "Can you come to New York? I want you to meet Count Basie and have him hear you sing."

I had never been on an airplane before, but that was no challenge for a Morehouse man. I mustered up all of my courage and entered the plane to be greeted by a very courteous stewardess, who directed me to my seat in the middle of the plane, not the rear. When we landed in New York, I was met by Basie's road manager. He drove me to the Hotel Theresa, which was known as "the Waldorf

Astoria of Harlem" and for years was the tallest building in the community.

The next morning, I was picked up and driven to an even taller skyscraper, the RCA building, or what is known as the GE building today, in Rockefeller Center. When I saw my driver push the button to the fifty-seventh floor, I realized it would be a serious ride. I was led into a plush reception area where a secretary gave me the yokel look, and advised me that Basie would see me shortly. 'What am I doing here?' I wondered. But I was determined to see it through.

After what seemed to be hours, but was probably only fifteen minutes, the secretary stood and said, "Mr. Basie will see you now." I was ushered into a room that looked like a Hollywood set, with modernist furniture, incandescent lighting around the walls, and a white baby grand in the middle. Basie was sitting at the piano and Hammond was on the sofa. They stood up to greet me and I was introduced as "the boy from Morehouse."

I was quite nervous but as the conversation drew on, I finally started to relax. We talked about Morehouse, and Basie started telling me about the road and his experiences in Kansas City, where he had developed his distinct brand of swing. He then asked me to sing a couple of songs for him. With hardly a pause, he proclaimed, "I think we got us a singer." That was it. And I was on Cloud Nine.

I told them I wanted to go back to school and finish the term, and they agreed that was a good idea. At home, my mom and sister were more excited than I was, but my dad needed some convincing. He had dreamed of me becoming a lawyer, but knew we didn't have money for law school. My proposal — a sincere one at that point — was that I would work with Basie for a couple of years if he would have me, save up sufficient funds and go back to school. And that's the only way I got a nod from my father.

My next grand experience was flying into the Atlanta airport courtesy of the Basie band and being greeted by my roommates and fraternity brothers. But Dr. Mays was a little more like my dad in the enthusiasm department.

"Good luck," he said, "but I think you would have made greater contributions as a lawyer than a singer."

Chapter 3

Big Times with Basie

The instructions were wired with my ticket: Go to the Hotel Theresa, check in and await further instructions. My first arrival had been met by a greeting and an escort. This time I was on my own.

I checked into my room, then went downstairs to find the restaurant and make a general survey of the hotel. I was immediately impressed with the fashionable dress of the women and sharp look of the men: tailored suits, white shirts, and shoes shined to such a mirror-finish you could see your face in them. You can imagine how I stood out with my Morehouse sweater, sweatshirt, duck pants, and loafers. Suddenly, I felt so alone and out of place. What was I doing here, in New York, with all of these strangers?

I peeked into the bar and noticed a familiar face. I had met a few of the band members on my previous visit, and this looked like one of them. As I approached, he recognized me and smiled. What a relief to see a warm, friendly Harry "Sweets" Edison, the trumpet player who had made a trademark of calling out during the Count's solos in a high, girlish voice, "Count Basie. Yeah, Count Basie. Play it, Count Basie."

We settled in to talk about the band and things I should be aware of, starting with the dress code. "Your school attire is OK for the road," he told me. "But when you come back to New York or play the major cities like Chicago, Los Angeles, or San Francisco, you dress up and look the part of a star — which is the way other people will look at you." A star? Was I going to be a star? At any rate, I liked the sound of it.

Count Basie's band had been riding high for more than ten years, ever since Hammond had visited Kansas City to check the group out in the summer of 1936. He was blown away by what he heard; an ensemble that could swing harder than any small group, or flair out into orchestral-sounding arrangements. Hammond shepherded them along, and the group recorded its signature theme, "One O'Clock Jump" in July 1937. Now I was getting to join this great tradition which had given rise to so many fantastic musicians, from Lester Young and Herschell Evans, to singers including Billie Holiday.

Early the next morning, I woke up to a phone call from Henry Snodgrass, my escort during the first visit. "I'll pick you up in one hour," he said. "Be dressed, packed, and checked out." My heart beat fast and strong with excitement. I made it downstairs in time. Good thing; Snodgrass was always on time. When I inquired about our itinerary, he said, "The band members are meeting the bus at the Apollo, and we depart in one hour for Philadelphia and the chitlin' circuit."

I knew chitlins, or chitterlings, were the soul food dish made of boiled pig intestines. But I had never heard of the chitlin' circuit, the name given to the string of theaters in black communities where black entertainers found their audiences in the segregated era. In Philly it was the Orpheum Theatre, and in Baltimore, the Royal. Chicago had the Regal, Washington DC had the Howard, and New York boasted the Apollo, the most famous of them all. The Basie band enjoyed the ability to travel back and forth between the segregated and non-segregated circles of the day, sometimes playing the black theater in one city and coming back on the next tour to play the white one.

As the band members gathered, I was introduced to them one-by-one. I tried to play it cool by not showing how thrilled I was at meeting the men whose names were on all those recording credits and black jazz magazines I had read. All I could think was, 'Now I am one of them.'

The Count was not on the bus. He was scheduled to meet the band in Philadelphia for a rehearsal prior to our opening day. I was anxious to know what numbers I was going to sing since I had no arrangements. The previous ballad singer, Earle Warren, was primarily a baritone, but had some arrangements that would fit my key and do until I got my own. Jimmy Rushing, "Mr. Five by Five," was the vocal star of the band who had been with Basie since 1928, when he and pianist Basie traveled with Walter Page and his Blue Devils. Rushing handled most of the jump-swing, shoutin' blues and novelty tunes. Helen Humes had been the band's female vocalist since 1938, and her signature songs included "Between the Devil and the Deep Blue Sea." I began to wonder where I fit in. I shared a dressing room with Jimmy and he let me know how rough the circuit audiences could be. "Watch out for those midnight shows on Saturday night. Those crowds are wild, and if they don't like you, they'll throw eggs at you."

Of course I made my debut at one of these midnight shows. But I learned I could put my faith in the Count. He had me sing my audition song, a Hugo Winterhalter arrangement of "Danny Boy." That's right, a black swing band doing an Irish ballad. But it stopped the show, and would continue to every time I sang it. I think the positive reaction to my debut also had a lot to do with Basie's special introduction: "Here's a young man who comes to us straight from Morehouse College in Atlanta, making his first appearance with us tonight."

One of the first items of Basie business was my new name. Bill Bailey, Pearl's brother, was the tap dancer who invented "the Backslide," what Michael Jackson would later call "the Moonwalk." He was hugely popular on the circuit, and occasionally billed with the Basie band on the road. To call me Bill Bailey would have created too much confusion on the marquees. Since the other Bill was a star and I was just a band singer, you can imagine who lost. They had to give me another name, and they gave me "Bob."

The chitlin' crowds seemed to like me. I never had eggs thrown in my direction. After the first round of the circuit with the old arrangements, I was promised some new material. I recorded "Danny Boy" as well as "I'm Drowning in Your Deep Blue Eyes" with the band in March 1947, and later took a crack at "Blue and Sentimental." At some of the first-class rooms and hotels such as the Waldorf Astoria, Helen and I were featured instead of Little Jimmy.

I was very fortunate to be with Basie during a period when he was working with some of the biggest stars in the business, and I was right there on the same bill. We were an act that was able to cross over from the chitlin' circuit to the top theaters.

I have warm memories of "Pops" Louis Armstrong and his words of encouragement: I would do very well if I was patient and stayed away from heavy drugs, but a little weed was okay, occasionally. It certainly was for him. He loved the weed. He was also a big fan of the herbal laxative "Swiss Kriss," which came in handy when you were traveling and eating different food. According to Pops, Swiss Kriss solved everything, and "keeps things flowing." He would laugh about taking it and then sitting on the toilet with a joint in hand. That was heaven!

The drugs weren't so innocuous for Billie Holiday. Helen Humes had replaced her as Basie's singer well before I joined the band, but Basie was billed with her again in New York at the Strand Theater, sharing the marquee with the premiere of the Humphrey Bogart-Lauren Bacall classic *Key Largo* in 1948. I had a chance to talk with her between shows, and wondered why such a wonderful person needed to indulge in this drug fantasy. I guess it was a reflection of her past lifestyle with overwhelming relationships and the inability to cope.

Our three-week contract at the Strand was extended for another week or two. During that long run, Billie got comfortable enough with me to shoot up while I was in the same room. We were talking one night, and she just started pulling out her little kit with a hypodermic needle, a spoon, and the dope. She put the dope in the spoon with a drop of water from the eyedropper, put it in the syringe and then she put it in her side. It was an experience I never, ever wanted to see again. But she just did it as a matter of fact, and even kept on talking while she was cooking and inserting it.

I told Basie about it and he said, "Well, you're one of the chosen few. She usually doesn't like anybody around when she's taking her fix." I don't think Billie felt she was doing anything that would upset me, or disrupt the conversation we were having. She knew I was aware she was on drugs, so what was the big deal?

But I was starry-eyed as far as just being around her and on the same show. She took a liking to me; not anything personal, but a professional liking because I think I was singing something different than the average crooner with a big band. Later on, after I left Basie, I was with the Clarence Robinson show in Philadelphia when she had a real binge and was going down very quickly. I was the emcee on the show, and had to help her onto, and sometimes off, the stage. But once you put her in front of a microphone, Billie didn't need you until she was through. She was a very warm, wonderful person and it was a travesty that she was taken advantage of by the men in her life.

We did a few gigs with Ella Fitzgerald, too. What a sweetheart. Combine her warm personality with an extraordinary vocal ability and you have a person you love to be around. Ella loved Basie and the band loved her, especially when she would match any instrument in a duel of solos with her scat-riffing. She was tops.

Dusty Fletcher and Pigmeat Markham were our two Vaudevillian comedians. They both transformed that era of comedy into situation sketches, and each man laid claim to the famous routine, "Open the Door, Richard." In 1947, the Basie band recorded one of several musical interpretations of the comedy sketch about a drunk trying to get his roommate to let him back into their apartment. One weekend, I actually got to work as Markham's straight man after his regular partner got ill. There were only two days to learn my lines and anticipate the correct timing. While I had some acting ability, I had no experience as a comic straight man, delivering lines to a pro like Pigmeat. Just before going on stage the first time, I felt like I was going to pee myself. I was nervous as hell. But something happens when your cue comes up. Pig was easy to work with, and I automatically responded to him and relaxed. My biggest problem was trying to keep a straight face when I looked at him. It was fun and a lot of work, at least for my three short days with a master showman.

On one stop at the W.C. Handy Theatre in Memphis, the Basie band shared the stage with the Will Mastin Trio. I had a dressing room down the hall from the group, and I heard this singing. It sounded so good, I said, "Who the hell is this?"

I came out of the dressing room, into the hallway and saw this little guy vocalizing. I was amazed. I said, "Are you on the show?"

"Yeah, I'm with the Will Mastin Trio."

That was my first introduction to Sammy Davis, Jr. I was glad when that engagement ended because he was fierce competition. I knew he was a dancer, but I didn't know he was a singer. We would cross paths again and become great friends who even tried to do business together, but that gets ahead of the story.

MOST OF MY BASIE MEMORIES ARE SORTED BY city. Producer-choreographer Ziggy Johnson promoted our two-month run at Club Paradise in Atlantic City, and he pulled all the swinger action from Detroit, his main base, for "an all-star sepia revue" with big production numbers, chorus girls, and comedians.

Johnson's biggest competitor, Larry Steele, also was in Atlantic City with a big show called "Smart Affairs." After our shows, the two casts had a fun time hanging out together. Big-number bankers, professional people, pimps, and ladies of the evening all mixed, let their hair down, and had a ball. But there was hell to pay at the end of the season. The undercover cops kept watch on those who smoked pot and snorted cocaine during the season. At the end of the engagement, they made a sweep with the paddy wagon and used city hall to process all of the people they rounded up. Most people paid their fines and were released. The dealers got a little more attention; one or two got thirty to sixty days in jail as an example. They were probably the ones who didn't pay off the cops. At least that was the scuttlebutt.

In Seattle, we played three nights in a ballroom that was packed every evening. For the guys in the band, the real excitement came from the ladies of the evening who would come down from Alaska to hear us play. They flashed their sexy evening wear, bought us drinks and, in some cases, provided warm relations for the evening. The working girls were not working for someone else's pleasure, but for their own. Needless to say, Seattle was a great engagement.

The RKO Golden Gate Theatre in San Francisco was a sophisticated contrast to Seattle. It was an easy gig because we played in the daytime and were off during the evening, free to roam the city. The black area of San Francisco was adjacent to downtown, supporting jazz clubs and restaurants. The guys in the band would sit in with the local acts and play to all hours of the morning. It was a great way to relax and get away from the charted music of the show. It also provided the chance to create new sounds and share new musical frontiers.

San Francisco also introduced me to the gay community. I remember hearing talk at home about one of my cousins, but it was all in a whisper. When they referred to him, they called him a sissy. He never bothered me, but I did notice he walked kind of funny, with sort of a swish. And he would put his hands on his hips when he was talking to make a point. In Frisco, it was a big contrast to see all the gays out in the open. One night, we noticed one of our post-show nightclub hangouts advertised "An

Evening with the Ladies." I looked forward to meeting someone I could have a conversation with, maybe a drink or two. This ladies' night was made to order.

After our last show, I couldn't wait to get to the club. When I got there the place was jamming, the lights were down low, and the smell of fried chicken filled the air. After making my way to the bar, I began to survey the crowd, looking for just the right person to talk to. To my surprise, I noticed some of the men were swishing. Then I started seeing the women, with some mighty big feet jammed into their high-heel shoes. What the hell was going on? My bar companion may have fooled me if I hadn't seen a beard growing under the makeup. I decided to stay cool. There must be some real ladies in the crowd. But I had to make a close inspection, or I might make a serious mistake.

My buddy had brought his mouthpiece for the trumpet so he could sit in and play with the band. After he played a few numbers, they called me up. I sang "Moonlight in Vermont" and "Someone to Watch Over Me." The audience swooned, but I couldn't handle the action. I went to the bar, had a couple of drinks, waved at my buddy and headed for the hotel. As I walked home, I thought about the old folks back home with their sissy talk, and decided I was happy that this community was really at peace with themselves, and couldn't care less what you whispered or said out loud.

Visiting Los Angeles for the first time is a once-in-a-lifetime thrill, especially if you grew up in an eastern city that denies you this kind of beauty. The smell of the ocean and the palm trees completely captured my imagination.

It made me remember my dreams on those snow-driven nights in Cleveland, when the temperatures would fall to ten below zero, of escaping to paradise. Well, I didn't have to dream anymore. I was in the land of dreams and I intended to enjoy it.

Our bus took us to the Dunbar Hotel on Central Avenue, home to all the action of black Los Angeles. A quick glance up and down the street revealed a number of clubs. My heart skipped a beat when I thought of starring in this town with Count Basie and enjoying the glances of some of the lovely ladies who would come to watch the show. After checking in, I thought I would walk the street and take an inventory of the nightspots: the Last Word, the Memo, the Downbeat, and Club Alabam, all within walking distance of the hotel. They all looked inviting and I intended to visit to all of them. Of course, the Alabam show had a line of beautiful dancers and I would probably spend most of my spare time — pardon me, quality time — backstage.

Our engagement was at the Fox Theatre and the band had received a great deal of publicity. My name was mentioned along with Jimmy Rushing and Ann Moore. The first show was very important, as the early birds and critics would spread the word, but we were ready for them and blew the roof off the theatre. We became the hottest thing in town; I couldn't wait to get to Central Avenue and see what they were saying about us.

The reports must have been good because everyone was smiling, from the bellman to the desk clerk. When I got to my room, I discovered an invitation to a reception at the Last Word cocktail lounge. A beautiful young lady welcomed me and placed a glass of champagne in my hand. The lounge had "Welcome Count Basie" signs on the walls and photos of some of the musicians, though Rushing was the only singer pictured. 'Next year, my picture will be on the wall — maybe, if I'm lucky,' I figured. At any rate, I was here, and with a high profile due to my performance at the theater.

I stood at the bar, and a young lady came over and started a conversation. Before long, we discovered she had gone to Clark College, the school across from Morehouse, and we had a lot in common. We even knew some of the same people in Atlanta. As I was about to invite her to the hotel to see my etchings, I was called upon to sing a song. After three or four numbers, I looked over and she was gone. She may have thought I had enough action and didn't want to compete, or simply enjoyed the conversation and that was that. At any rate, she was gone.

The next few nights I explored some of the other clubs on the Central Avenue Strip. One of the ladies I had met with "Sweets" Edison one evening agreed to meet me after the show for a drink and a late snack. She suggested we go to Stuff Crouch's, which was an after-hours joint that opened when the regular clubs closed. All of the stars who were playing in town would meet there and socialize until daybreak. Everything on the menu was exorbitant as far as price, but it didn't matter because that's where the celebrities wined and dined.

I was impressed with the atmosphere and the music. However, the little snack my date talked about ended up being a porterhouse steak accompanied by a bottle of champagne. I was bowled over when I got the bill. It was horrendous, much more than I had in my pocket. I started to panic. Just in the nick of time, Basie came in and greeted me. I quickly took him aside.

"I might not be singing tomorrow night because I might be in jail. I don't have enough money to pay this bill."

He laughed and said, "Don't worry about it." The waitress came by and informed our table, "Mr. Basie's picking up the check," which made me really seem like a big shot. Sure it came out of my pay, but that little detail was between him and me. Basie was kind of like a dad. You could go to him and talk about anything. But I had learned my lesson: Stay away from stage doors unless you can pay the price for a midnight snack! The next night I visited alone, and enjoyed a house salad and a glass of wine.

Paul Gonsalves came in as the new tenor saxophonist about the same time I started, and we were paired as roommates because we were equally naïve in terms of our experience on the road. There were a lot of drugs in some of the other bands, like Dizzy Gillespie's. But the Basie band members were older, seasoned musicians and they kept their arms around the youngsters in the group. They used to call me "Schoolboy."

In Salt Lake City, some of us had to sleep in a whorehouse or stay in the homes of the few black families that lived there because the hotel where we played did not accommodate our people. Segregation was nationwide, but the difference was that most cities with large black populations had built-up communities and you didn't feel it as much. But a great audience and a night in a whorehouse made things a little easier to bear.

We traveled mostly by train when it was possible, but took buses on the one-night tours of towns that didn't always have train service. Some of the new buses already had sleeping accommodations; older members of the band would use the bunks, leaving the younger among us to folding-back chairs. A couple of the band members were very light-skinned, so when we stopped for sandwiches we would send them in. Otherwise, they would often charge us more for being a black group. If they looked white enough to the beholder, we didn't mind playing on people's racist attitudes to our financial benefit.

In Chicago, every restaurant had good soul food at reasonable prices. I could afford to buy a "snack" for a date in this town. The Pershing Hotel had a cabaret in the basement, which featured variety shows and a chorus line of beautiful girls. This club competed with another "black show" at the famous jazz joint Club DeLisa. Chicago was next to New York for having a great mixture of jazz, swing, and blues. They say Memphis had the best barbecue, but whenever Chicago was on our itinerary, I abstained from eating ribs because I was sure to get my fill in the Windy City.

Our engagement was at the Oriental Theater downtown, a mostly white audience that reversed the ratio of our shows at the Regal, our uptown stop on the chitlin' circuit. We played both, sometimes in the same year. The show was a little groovier at the Regal, while the Oriental was a little more straight-laced. Downtown or uptown, we always headed for the action on the Southside after the show.

This was the home of the Step Brothers, so I had a chance to get acquainted with the famous tap dance team that had been vaudeville stars since the late 1920s. I spent more time seeing the town with the Step Brothers co-founder Al Williams because he was single, but I kept my feet ready to go to newer member Prince Spencer's dining room table, as his wife, Gerri, was some kind of a cook. When Gerri put on a spread, you were in for a treat. She was at home with every Southern dish you could think of: greens, macaroni and cheese, fried okra, sweet potatoes, pigs' feet, chitterlings, and of course, cornbread. Years down the road, Prince and I would share Las Vegas as our home address.

Another highlight of Chicago nightlife was the house parties. One of the local bookies would always throw a party for Basie and the band which was a treat compared to those clubs where they had their hands in your pockets. The main attraction was usually straight corn whiskey, one hundred-and-whatever proof, and I know it was illegal booze because it never had a label on the bottle. The fact that you could not purchase it in a liquor store made it more of a curiosity for the party. By the way, you didn't wake up with a headache the next day. You might wake up in a strange bed, but never with a headache.

My favorite town to visit, of course, was Atlanta. I was the famous Morehouse man coming home as a star with a famous band. Basie would always let me sing more songs so I could show off. He would do that for all the performers, let us have some extra attention in our hometowns or places where we had a special connection. He really pushed me out front when we played the theater in

Cleveland. Dad and Mom would walk around with their chests out for the entire week of our engagement. Basie was at the peak of his fame, and my coming out of public housing and singing with Count Basie was a big thing.

Dad had been the only one hesitant about me joining the band. He still wished I had gone to law school, his dream for me, but once I was in my second year with the band, it became evident that law school was getting further and further away. At first when I played at home, Dad would mention school. Eventually, I guess he resigned himself to having a singing son as opposed to a lawyer. It could have been worse, and he knew I was happy with a song in my heart.

But things were drying up for the big bands in the late 1940s. They were too expensive to maintain and do-wop was starting to take over pop music, while modern jazz and hard bop became the fascination of jazz buffs. Basie took a vacation to contemplate his future and regroup, reducing the band to a small group of seven musicians with just one singer, Jimmy Rushing. He was a part of some of the band's biggest recordings and the fans would be looking for him.

It was time for me to move on and begin the next chapter. And by this time, I was dead set on someone I wanted to spend my future chapters with, side-by-side.

Chapter 4

Anna

So far, you might have noticed that many of my life's decisions were at least in part about women, or at least the pursuit of them. But now, as the train pulls out of the station from Chicago to take the Basie band back to New York, it's only about one.

I lean back, close my eyes, and remember the prettiest girl I have ever seen. My thoughts drift back to the first time I saw her.

The Basie band was playing at a Broadway hot spot called the Aquarium, and the girls in the show at the nearby Zanzibar Club would come over between their shows to catch one of our sets. One of the girls knew my friend Buddy Tate, and she dropped in with a friend —Anna Porter. After the set came the intermission and my opportunity to be introduced. We approached their table. As she shook my hand, her smile was warm and sincere. Needless to say, I was impressed, and wanted to talk. But they had to get back to their show. Oops, I forgot to even ask for her phone number. 'Maybe the show would still be at the Zanzibar the next time we come back to New York,' I told myself without really believing it. I was really kicking myself for not getting the number. Oh well. A girl that pretty probably had a boyfriend already. And many more potential ones running after her. I would just be one little band singer joining the crowd. Still, somehow I knew I would see her again.

I didn't have to wait too long. Cincinnati was the third Ohio stop on a bus tour of one-nighters for the band. The bus rolled into Cincinnati about 3 AM on the day of our show. Chatting with the desk clerk, we discovered the Zanzibar show was playing across the river in Covington, Kentucky and the girls were staying at our hotel. I inquired as to whether or not a friend of mine, Winnie Benson, was registered. The clerk checked, said yes, and gave me the room number. It helped that I told him she was my cousin. I checked into my own room, then decided to find Winnie's to say hello.

After a few knocks on the door, Winnie answered all bleary-eyed. It wasn't the warmest welcome, as you might suspect at that hour, but we managed a brother-and-sister-type hug. Then I noticed another person sleeping on a cot in the room. As she turned to face us, Winnie started to introduce us. It was Anna. Of course I remembered her, but she acted as if she was seeing me for the first time. I guess that told me how much of an impression I had made on her when we had met a few months before in New York. I invited the girls to the last set of the last show and maybe some breakfast afterward.

I was excited and full of anticipation, but told myself, 'Be cool. Act unaffected.' As luck would have it, Winnie knew other people in the band and I didn't have to host her for breakfast. I had Anna all to myself. I took the family approach and started laying on a lot of trivia about my past, and learned a little about her in the process.

Anna was born in Georgia, but her mother moved her to Hoboken, New Jersey and then Brooklyn by the time she was a year old. She attended the East New York Vocational High School, but — much like me with the singing — her dancing had guided her away from academics. Watching the way she would swirl around after coming home from a Fred Astaire movie, her mother decided to put her in dance classes. At first they were just a childhood game to her, but by age ten she was taking them seriously. By the time she was thirteen or fourteen, Anna already had grown to a height of five-foot six. Her entrée into show business had come when the girls on the chorus line of the famous Apollo Theater in Harlem went on strike, and the management turned to Anna's dance school to recruit fill-ins for that week. "Almost all of the junior high came to see me," she told me. "I was so big when I went back to school."

By then she had the fever, and was rarely out of work as a professional dancer from then on. It was tough to finish high school, getting home at 2 or 3 AM and then getting rousted by her mom to get to school three hours later. "I was pretty good at falling asleep in school," she told me. "I would do it behind a book, or pretend to faint so I could go lay down for half an hour in the nurse's office. But I was just so intrigued with being in the business and being around all the stars then."

When she was sixteen, she packed a little bag and left home to go to California with the chorus line of a revue called *Born Happy*, starring Bill "Bojangles" Robinson. But after a month, she got homesick and left that show, paying a $500 fine to the Associated Guild of Variety Artists in order to come back home. After that, Anna had been able to stay close to home, thanks to the many black revues on Broadway or in Harlem. When one closed, another would open and she would perform in green velvet costumes costing $350 to $500 each, backing the likes of Cab Calloway. When she was old enough to really enjoy it, she did get to go to Europe as one of four girls picked to travel with swing star Louis Jordan, who had made inroads into segregated radio and was known as "King of the Jukebox." But more often, she would take the subway to clubs in Harlem or Manhattan, then home again, often greeting the dawn at 5 AM in her wide hat and white gloves.

In turn, I told her about my Morehouse days, and what I intended to do with my life after Basie. I wanted to impress upon her that I was going to be someone someday, and would need a good woman on my arm. Suddenly, I caught myself, realizing I was getting a little too serious a little too soon.

Seeing Anna yawn a couple of times drove home the realization that it was getting late. I wanted to keep talking until dawn, but alas, she told me it was time to turn in. I offered to walk her to her room. When we arrived, she kissed me on the cheek, told me what a nice time she had, handed me her Brooklyn telephone number and said good night. As I walked to my room, I rubbed the cheek she had kissed and felt glad I didn't suggest any hanky panky. I think that would have blown it. All would come in good time.

AFTER COUNT BASIE DECIDED TO DOWNSIZE his group, I was invited to do a solo engagement by producer Baron Wilson at Small's Paradise on Seventh Avenue, one of the big three nightclubs in Harlem. The money was not what I felt I was worth, but it was my first booking as a single and it might lead to others. Either way, it would keep me working under contract four weeks. The club really rolled out the star treatment; Norma Miller had the house dancers build a great number around me. They advertised for three weeks before opening night, which was coincidentally about the exact amount of time I had calculated my bank account would hold out.

I found an apartment on Morningside and 123rd Street. In this part of Harlem you didn't just rent an apartment, you had to buy the lease from the current tenant and then pay a transfer fee to put the lease in your name. Everyone hustled you, but that's the way it was. After I bargained for furniture and added a few personal touches, I settled into my first real address since college, christening the place in a couple of the weekend gatherings with some of old buddies from Morehouse.

Almost two months slipped by before I realized I had not called Anna. All of my memories flashed before me and I rubbed my face where she had kissed me that night in Cincinnati. Eager to call, I realized my little black book did not reveal her name. Somehow, I forgot to transfer it to the address book after that night in Cincinnati. I called my friend, Buddy Tate, to get the number of his friend who was with Anna the first time we were introduced at the Aquarium. Buddy went to work and called back in the hour with the telephone number. I had to promise not to tell Anna how I got the number from her girlfriend. But I was back in business. I called. When she answered, I got a lump in my throat.

"Bet you don't know who this is calling you?" She didn't catch my voice and I figured I'd better stop playing and tell her who it was before she hung up. Her response was warm. After a few moments of chitchat, I pushed for a date. She responded by inviting me to her house. She still lived at home in Brooklyn. Brooklyn! That might as well have been a foreign country to me. I had just begun to feel comfortable finding my way around Harlem, but it didn't matter. "Brooklyn, here I come."

I got on the phone and called my Morehouse buddy Bootsie, who knew all the boroughs, and asked him to go with me. He agreed and I started to make preparations for a romantic visit. I laid out my sharpest clothing. But you can't set a romantic scene without music. I had my own copy of Gordon Jenkins' *Manhattan Tower*, one of the earliest experiments in full-length albums and made to romantic order. I called to make sure she had a record player that would play it. No, her mother's player could only handle the old single 78s. No problem, I would bring my portable and the records.

Friday seemed like it would never come, but that morning finally found me anxiously waiting for Bootsie to arrive. He had warned me to dress warm, because Brooklyn was even colder than Harlem. The subway seemed awfully slow, and we were jostling for space with the record player and case, loaded with Basie and romantic vocals. It was a long ride, but we finally made the Stuyvesant Street stop. Now we only had to walk eight of the longest blocks in the world. Finally we got to the house, a big fourteen-room brownstone with a porch stoop and everything you would see in the movies. (I soon learned her mom and stepfather, a landscaper and tree doctor, barely made ends meet. They occupied the bottom two floors and rented the top two out to boarders.) I rang the doorbell and there she was, smiling and gorgeous. Keeping my cool, I introduced my buddy and we went in.

Things got off to a good start on what was supposed to be a daylong visit; we arrived about 10 AM and planned to leave after dinner, around 9 PM. We were having such a good time, we didn't pay much attention to the snow falling outside. Eventually, we realized more than six inches covered the street and the snow was still coming down steadily. We turned on the radio for a weather report, which predicted a blizzard of three to four feet by midnight. It would be impossible for us to get to the subway station by walking. Cabs were out of the question. We would have to stay overnight.

I never enjoyed bad weather so much.

Fortunately, Anna's mother made us comfortable on the couch and the one guest bedroom. Little did I know, the storm would last for three days. It would take another day still to begin the cleanup of the streets and sidewalks. But good things can come of any bad situation. Being snowed in gave me the opportunity to bond with Anna, and share some time with her mother. I think her mom liked me, even as she wondered if we would ever leave. Anna remembers that she kept hearing the refrigerator door opening, and complaining, "They're cleaning us out!"

By the time we left, I made a commitment to myself that I was going to marry this girl. I knew I would have competition, but figured I could hold my own. But for now, I had to get back to the gig at Small's. When I had called and explained the situation, they closed for the three days of the blizzard. Moreover, I was getting good reviews, doing good business and they liked me enough to hold me over for another four weeks, with more money.

I developed a friendship with one of the acts on the show, a dancer everyone knew as "Johnny Tap." After the show, we would hang out at an after-hours joint named Johnny Walker's. It didn't open until 4 AM when the other clubs closed, so all the entertainers and showgirls headed there on their way home. Some after-hours clubs operated out of private houses, but this was a big one with a dance floor and a regular bar.

That, plus my memories of Stuff Crouch's, the after-hours operation run by Basie's friend of that name in California, set my entrepreneurial wheels into motion. What if I ran a little club of my own? Johnny Tap was well known in the Harlem nightlife. If I could get Anna to bring some of her girlfriends, I would have a good package and we could compete. Johnny was encouraging, assuring that he would handle the juice necessary to operate as a private club.

We found a great apartment on "The Hill," 143rd and Amsterdam, not too far from Johnny Walker's. We rounded up some couches to place throughout the apartment, did some quick decorating to convert the kitchen into a bar area and lined up a lone cocktail waitress. In no time we had a cozy little club with a capacity for maybe 40 people, and were ready to kick off with a grand opening. The word spread quickly among the various shows working in Harlem to come down on a free invitation the first night and help get us off the ground.

Everything went great and it was evident that we were pulling some of Johnny Walker's business. Being the star of my own show made it easy to promote myself as an after-hours attraction. However, I was not fully savvy on how the game was played in New York or how Johnny Tap had arranged our private club license.

On Saturday night of our third weekend, the police busted us. They barged in and told everyone, "Go home or go to jail." I was very indignant, fully convinced that we were operating legitimately. "We have a private club license," I told him. The captain asked to see it. I looked for Johnny and discovered he had disappeared. I began to get nervous, realizing I had taken a position I couldn't back up. As the place emptied out, he pulled me aside. "Don't you know Johnny Walker is the only one who can operate in this area?"

It turned out that Walker paid the police enough to enforce his status as the only operator in that part of Harlem. Anybody else who wanted a piece of the after-hours action had to go through him. We hadn't done that, and we were taking his business. So he put the pressure on the department, which he had been paying off to stay in business. The Captain indicated he would not take me downtown if I would make a donation to the Policemen's Benefit League. I knew right away it was a way of asking for money without incriminating himself by asking for a shakedown. I gave him the night's take. And that was the end of my New York business venture.

I saw Johnny the next day and asked him about his timely disappearance. He said he had gotten ill and left, but didn't want to disturb me during a deep conversation. He also insisted he had paid one of the police captains to protect us: "I tell you, I don't know what happened!" Johnny probably had indeed paid someone, I figured, but the cop he paid apparently didn't talk much with the one who visited last night. Needless to say, this episode ended our relationship. But at that point, it was time to move on anyway. I was in my last two weeks at Small's Paradise and had been so distracted starting the club that I hadn't pursued any new bookings.

Fortunately, my old mentor John Hammond came through with a phone call on the morning of my last day. Would I be interested in trying out for a part in a theater musical staged in Hollywood? It was almost as unbelievable as the day he asked me to audition for the Basie band.

I started practicing to piano arrangements of my two best songs. The audition got off to a good start with a relaxing conversation with the producer. I already knew the piano player, and we skated through the first song. We were about to start the second when the producer said, "I've heard enough." I didn't think I was that bad! But neither did he: "The part is yours if we can get together on the money."

I asked how long the engagement would be. "With any luck, we'll last there a year and then be able to bring it back here to Broadway." This was great news, except for one thing: Anna. We were starting to get very close. The thought of leaving Anna for a long stretch took some of the joy out of my good news. But show business is a hard taskmaster, and you go where it leads you, especially when you're trying to work your way up. So what should I do? Ask her to marry me.

Today, Anna tells our friends, "He always talked to me about marriage. He was always talking about our life together, what we're going to do, that he had potential and wanted to take me with him." But she also remembers that I had a little extra incentive to pop the question.

Anna was working at Club 845 in the Bronx, and I had gone to see her there enough times to know the way in. But one night, I wasn't able to talk my way inside. "Closed for a private party," they told me. The club was having a private get-together for Alice Key. Like Anna, she started out as a dancer in black revues, but she was one of our early activists. Alice had lobbied to improve dancer pay at the Cotton Club and organized a protest of a drug store that wouldn't hire blacks. She had given up dancing to start a second career as a journalist in 1943.

But Alice was back in town now, and that was a big enough deal for her entertainer friends from the old days to throw her a party. There must have been some pretty big names in there, because I was held at bay outside. Not only did I not have the juice to get in, Anna didn't even have the juice to vouch for me. She came to check on me a few times, but she stayed inside so long I was furious — mainly because I wasn't alone out there. There was another fellow waiting for Anna too. Today, she maintains he wasn't a boyfriend, just a friend of the family. But, she also says today, "I think I got my proposal promptly after that."

We agreed to save some money for our new life together, and to plan a wedding date either in Los Angeles or New York, depending on the success of the show. Of course I needed an engagement ring. My bank account was not too healthy, but I had to make a showing. So I took half of my savings, about $300, and ended up getting a ring that was about a third of a carat — small, but full of fire! Anna spared me the brutal details at the time, but later confessed that when she showed the ring to her dancer girlfriends, they teased her and asked, "Is that the baby ring?" But she knew it was the best I could do at the time. With our engagement locked and my furniture sold, it was off to California.

❦

THE NAME OF THE PLAY WAS *SUGAR HILL*. IT HAD started out in 1931 as a Broadway musical vehicle for the hit vaudeville team of Flournoy Miller and Aubrey Lyles, a follow-up to the first black Broadway hit *Shuffle Along*, which also incorporated Miller and Lyles. The original musical — a comic murder mystery about the upscale Harlem neighborhood of the title — only lasted eleven performances on Broadway. But Miller dusted it off and revised it twice, first in 1947 and then in June of 1949, with the subtitle *Meet Miss Jones*. This revival was staged at Hollywood's Las Palmas Theatre and directed by Charlie O'Curran, who would later marry actress Betty Hutton in Las Vegas.

For a guy who was used to the looseness of jazz musicians and the nightclub scene, it was intimidating to be around all these theater pros. I had to revamp my musical and physical posture to sing and dance with an emphasis on the lyric. And I had not had to memorize or deliver lines since I was in high school plays.

My role as the juvenile lead partnered me with a lovely young lady with a soprano voice like a bird. She was the ingénue, and it was clear that I would have to belt out my songs and forget being a balladeer. When this girl threw a musical line to you — and boy could she belt it — you had to respond in kind.

Opening night brought a sold-out house and the critics, but the cast was ready to go. We performed with flawless timing and comedic flair. I was just proud to be a part of it all. Adhering to Broadway tradition, we waited up all night for the reviews. When the newspapers arrived, we watched as the director read the first one. His face was stern, he lifted his brow, and at the last minute, he smiled and said, "It's a hit!"

The elation faded into the realization that we were going to have to work hard to keep that opening night energy going for seven shows per week, including a Saturday afternoon matinee. But for the next few months, I saw a different side of Los Angeles than the one I did with the Basie band. I was running with another group: the Hollywood types, not the jazz buffs or swing crowd. But I also looked up some contacts I had made with the band, and enjoyed being able to feel somewhat at ease amid both groups. The Hollywood crowd entertained in their lavish homes. The jazz people stuck to the clubs. I had considered myself basically a crooner, a balladeer. But my voice training at Morehouse and my limited exposure to the classics paid off with these Hollywood invitations.

The producers had figured that success in Los Angeles would land them a Broadway theater after about six months. But as the half-year mark approached, Broadway had yet to take the bait, perhaps not realizing how much times in general, and *Sugar Hill* in particular, had changed since its first Broadway flameout. Their only option at that point was to negotiate an extension in Los Angeles for another four months. Those months came and went with still no theater deal for New York, so the show had to close.

I missed Anna, but also wanted to pursue work in the California nightspots, or audition for bit parts in movies. I asked her if she wanted to come out West, but she wasn't interested. I told her I would try out some potential opportunities, and if they didn't work out, I would be back to New York in a couple of weeks.

A couple of weeks grew into two months, then three months. One day, the doorbell rang. The postman had a special delivery for Bob Bailey. I wondered who would send me such an important-looking package. It was stamped from New York. The first thing I read was the letter.

"You evidently have found reasons to stay in Los Angeles. I am sending you back your engagement ring and the bankbook with our savings (the money you sent). I wish you good luck and good-bye. — Anna."

I was crushed; my world fell apart as I looked at the ring, the bankbook and the letter, which I read over and over again.

Suddenly, the opportunities of California meant nothing if I was going to lose Anna. Win, lose, or draw, I knew it was time to get back to New York. As expected, my arrival was not greeted with a great display of joy. I knew I would have to renew the relationship at an arm's length in order to rekindle the fires of love and compassion. So be it.

"HE WAS SENDING THE MONEY. HE WAS SENDING almost all of his salary back. He was very good at that," Anna recalls now. "But he stayed a long time. I had heard rumors that maybe he was occupied a little bit. Show business is a small little family. It's a small world. You get a little information back about some of his adventures.

His intentions were good, but three thousand miles is a long way away.

"Really, I think I just didn't want to wait too long. During that time, I was pretty popular too, and I had a few proposals. I didn't know whether he was coming back or not, so I just decided to send everything back and to end it right there so I could go on with my life."

But Anna hadn't spent one cent of the money that was to be our combined savings. Even though we were both very young, she had the wisdom not to rush into a marriage unless I was really serious. I realized she couldn't stay mad forever. "Bob was always a talker," she says now. "You would see something, and he could talk and say, 'You didn't see a thing. I was just holding her hand, taking her to someone else.' He was charming and really glib of tongue. I think I just loved him from the minute I saw him."

ANNA WASN'T SURE WHAT TO MAKE OF ME, BUT her mother still loved me. And because her Brooklyn brownstone had rooms for rent, I asked if she would rent one to me.

After some reluctance and a private conversation with Anna, she relented and offered a small room. It wasn't the essence of luxury, but it would do for the time being. Now I had two goals: Find work and refurbish my love life. I let all of the old contacts know I was available, and could now be billed as "direct from Hollywood."

After a couple of weeks, I got a few calls. The best offer was from the same Club 845 that once had kept me waiting outside in the Bronx. The job called for a singer and emcee. I had never been a professional emcee, but with my recent experience in California, I felt it would be easy to introduce people, sing a few songs and bring some class to the show. The money was good and I started to get comfortable with hosting.

After three months, the owners wanted a new show. We were put on a two-week notice. Once again, I put the word out that I was available and landed work in a seven-member troupe at a club called La Vie En Rose. But it was starting to become apparent just how unpredictable show business was, and how some of the nightclubs were disappearing. It wasn't real bad yet, but you could see the handwriting on the wall. The post-War era had created the suburbs, a new period of "cocooning," as they would call it now, and the dawn of television. The show business I knew would have a gradual but inevitable decline over the next ten years. With this new thing called television, I decided that if you can't beat 'em, join 'em.

I talked all this over with the bass player in our revue, Leonard Gaskin. He agreed on all fronts, but what were we going to do about it? Do some research and find out how to get in. Leonard spotted a newspaper ad for The School of Radio and Television, offering courses in TV production and direction. We immediately called to get the information.

SRT, as it was known, operated out of offices at 57th and Broadway. Though Columbia University would eventually usurp it, SRT was one of the first schools to pull top talents from both radio and motion pictures and marry the two industries together. Our musical and theatrical background was a good foundation. Perhaps more important was that the school was colorblind to anything but green. Tuition was expensive, but we looked at it as an investment in our future.

I became a fulltime student, taking day and night classes while still holding down my job in the nighclub revue at La Vie En Rose. Leonard and I were the only black students. It was exciting to be fully accepted on the basis of our talent, something that concerned these show business professionals more than the color of our skin.

For the next few months, we learned the technical side of television production along with the on-camera skills of writing and interviews. We had to work the soundboard, spin records, and prepare lighting and camera coverage for various types of shows. To graduate, we had to hand in a complete show proposal. The teaching staff would review the submissions and choose one news show and one variety show to be performed as a class project. My variety show, a documentary called "The Evolution of Jazz," got the nod. I contacted some of the boys from the Basie band, and the whole class threw its energy into the production, with me directing and doing the announcements from the sound booth. It went over big!

Graduation requirements also included a third-class telephone operator's license, something you had to have back then to work the board at a radio station. With all this in hand, along with my experience in nightclubs and stage shows, I felt like some smart network would be lucky to get me first. I asked one of my instructors for some help in getting some interviews. He agreed, but he was getting ready to move back to Hollywood, where he was much better known than he was in New York. Still, he was able to put together two interviews: one at CBS and one a local CBS affiliate. The first one caught the interviewer off guard. I don't think he had been pre-warned that I was black. "We've heard really great things about your work," he told me, "but we're not looking for anyone at the moment." During an interview that must have lasted all of five minutes, he never looked me in the eye once. In fact, most of the time he looked down at the floor.

As I left the office, the reality hit home. I had been so wrapped up in schoolwork and the club job, so accepted by the staff of SRT, that I had not taken time to consider the fact that job discrimination might be prevalent in this new industry. But this was no time to get discouraged. I prepared for the next appointment at the local affiliate, hoping it would be better.

This interview was much more comfortable and informative. But we ran into a chicken-or-egg thing: My interviewer said stations were looking for experience, and I said you couldn't get experience without getting a foothold in the industry. He acknowledged my frustration, saying the unions were the culprits. "Maybe you could break into the business by getting into one of their apprentice programs," he suggested. He also noted that Columbia University was developing a TV production course at the encouragement of the networks, who were at the mercy of the unions and concerned about a strike. If I got into the class, maybe I could meet some of the movers and shakers in the industry. It was a good idea. Anything that would get me in was a good idea.

The class lasted for three months. I already knew almost as much as the teachers, thanks to SRT. But the real motivation for being there paid off. Most of the students were executives from the networks. Some of them were very slow in grasping a camera and sound equipment, but they weren't trying to become experts. They just needed to know enough to keep the network on the air during emergencies — or union negotiations.

I waited a long time for my classmates to notice how much I knew. Finally, I approached the two who had been the friendliest, both vice presidents from different networks. Each one said to call them and get hooked up with their personnel department. At last, I felt like I had something going. My mother had always told me, "Strike while the iron is hot."

I called the next week, hoping my name was still fresh in their minds. The guy from CBS had his secretary tell me she was setting up an appointment with personnel, and would call. The NBC guy never did call, but it was OK — the CBS secretary came through; no need to be greedy. I was excited, because I knew my friend had put in a good word.

I showed up for the interview with a resume and presentation package from SRT. I dressed conservatively, but with a little showbiz flair. The interviewer greeted me warmly and said my friend had spoken very highly of me. After a half an hour of chitchat about my stint with Count Basie and the rest, I asked, "What do the possibilities look like for me joining the TV effort at CBS?"

He became very businesslike and said there were no openings in the production staff. "But I promise to keep you in mind for the first opening that comes up." In the meantime, he was going to refer me to the tech division. I knew this would be a waste of time. We learned at SRT the tech department required a first-class operator's license. I had been treated courteously, but I understood: No license, no union membership, no hire. By now I was getting frustrated and angry. After all the money and time I had spent in school, plus my show experience, I just wanted an opportunity to demonstrate what I was capable of doing. Let me start at the bottom. Give me some job that only required muscle, such as a dolly pusher, who pushed the cameraman around. I would even be a page, seating the studio audience for live shows. But the former was another union job. And the latter? They said I was overqualified.

I called my agent to tell him I was once again available for nightclub work.

ANNA AND I FINALLY TIED THE KNOT IN February of 1951. My family was able to travel from Cleveland for a traditional afternoon wedding in a Catholic church in Brooklyn. The ceremony may have been typical, but the reception was not. Because we were both working — Anna in the Village and me in the Bronx — we threw the reception at 2 AM, after all our dancer, singer and chorus-girl friends got off work for the night. Among those sharing in the drinks and soul food was James Edwards, the black actor who had defied stereotypes of the day with his role in the 1949 World War II drama, *Home of the Brave*.

Anna and I worked steadily, sometimes together, sometimes apart. We were able to spend a couple of summers working for producer Clarence Robinson, hosting his variety revue in Philadelphia at the Paradise, the same club I had worked with the Basie band. The stage extended out into the audience, so I brushed up on some Yiddish songs to work the heavily Jewish patrons.

One could do much worse than working late, hanging out with the performers in the rival revue — still Larry Steele's *Smart Affairs* — then having champagne and peaches on the beach at daybreak before sleeping the rest of the day away.

I tried to shop my variety show to the Atlantic City TV station, but they didn't yet have the technical capabilities. The station manager seemed to like me though, and would drop by the club to talk about the TV industry. He felt trapped, with no upward mobility unless he went to New York or Atlantic City. I listened, trying to be sympathetic, but wishing I had even his job. The grass is always greener....

Atlantic City was a fine place for newlyweds, though we had some moments as all young marrieds do. One night I came home from a long night with the fellows with lipstick on my collar. Alcohol had kind of obliterated any memory of how it got there; probably just a tourist saying how much she enjoyed the show. Boy, did I catch it. By the time Anna finished with me, I was stone sober and forever apologetic.

Anna probably felt more secure when it was her turn to travel with Louis Jordan, and leave me alone with her mom. We were still living in her mom's house, and when I wasn't performing somewhere beyond the subway route, I looked forward to her good cooking and sitting home with her, playing cards.

When Anna got back, Clarence Robinson was able to put us in a show together, with her in the dance line and me as the singing emcee. The show opened to standing room only in Buffalo. This promised to be a great engagement and the working conditions were very good. After getting the show up and working out the rough patches every new effort has, Clarence started leaving town a lot. He was working on something big, but he wouldn't spill any information. What was he up to? Finally, he confided: "It's a show for Las Vegas, and it's almost a done deal."

Clarence wanted me to take charge of the show in Buffalo so he could close the deal and start the rehearsals in New York. He signed the contract and a new show was born: *Tropi-Can-Can*, a red-hot revue with new music, new costumes, and beautiful girls. The show was going to open a brand new hotel in Las Vegas called the Moulin Rouge. It was going to be the first integrated hotel in a town which would come to be known as the "Mississippi of the West," because its main industry, gambling, was segregated in order to curry to the players from the South and Midwest. The Moulin Rouge was at least going to take advantage of "separate but equal," with a budget as lavish as any other hotel in town.

Rehearsals started in New York in February 1955. The girls were hand-picked from more than one hundred who auditioned. Of course, they were all from the East, so Clarence decided to have more auditions in Los Angeles, where he could hire a third of them to cut down on his transportation costs. He ended up with a final count of twenty-seven dancers and showgirls, plus ten male dancers and a twenty-piece band directed by Benny Carter.

Anna left early; I stayed to close down the show in Buffalo. While the others would rehearse on site, I wasn't needed until two weeks before the show's scheduled opening in early May. Because we hoped to be in Vegas for a while, we agreed I should drive our new 98 Olds to Vegas. It would be fun to drive through Cleveland and spend a few days with the family. Of course, I wanted to show off my new car. Local boy makes good, and all that. And now the local boy was heading to yet another place he had never been before.

CHAPTER 5

The Moulin Rouge: A New Beginning

THERE'S A STORY ANNA TELLS ABOUT A TIME, not long after she arrived in the spring of 1955 to start rehearsals at the Moulin Rouge, when the sky dropped chunks of hail so dirty it looked as if the heavens were pitching rocks. Perhaps she thought it was just one more bit of tomfoolery, one more piece of mischief from the same fate that landed her in the middle of this strange little desert outpost.

Even on the day of her arrival, things were not as they seemed. She flew out from New York City with about a dozen of the East Coast dancers, all of them dressed to kill in hats and gloves, earrings and crimson-colored lipstick. As they got closer to Las Vegas, she spotted the lights of the city through her window, a tiny flicker hemmed in by miles and miles of dark, empty desert. She shook her head, wondering, "Is this it? Is this the 'Entertainment Capital of the World' I'd heard so much about? The one Pearl Bailey said was *the* place to be?"

At McCarran Airport, the girls were greeted by TV and newspaper photographers as if they were celebrities, then lined up for photos on the steps of the airplane's ramp, behind producer Clarence Robinson and Moulin Rouge financier Alexander Bisno who shook hands for the usual "grip-and-grin" photo used to publicize any new show in town. The girls were then loaded into limousines and buses, settling in for what they assumed was a short drive to the Strip where they had imagined themselves dancing. They didn't realize it was the last place in the world an integrated casino would ever take root.

As the drivers took them past the Strip, past Fremont Street, and underneath a traffic bridge they would later nickname the "Iron Curtain," the young women looked at one another with a mixture of disbelief and foreboding as if to say, "Well, here we go again. Here we are."

Arriving in town a few weeks later, my initial reaction also was one of dismay. A policeman on downtown Fremont Street gave directions to the Westside, the area set aside for Las Vegas' minority community, which consisted of blacks and a few Hispanics. As I drove down the dirt path that was "D" Street, small shacks and outhouses came into view on either side of the road. My heart sank. I would later learn that the creation of the Westside was a business decision by the movers and shakers who said they wanted to preserve their downtown land for expansion projects. But there was no doubt the action also was racially motivated.

Things got better once I turned onto Van Buren, then finally made my way to Berkley Square, a brand-new subdivision of nice one-story homes designed by African American architect Paul Williams and marketed to the black community in anticipation of the area's growth. While the surrounding neighborhoods were threaded through with rock and mud, the minute you hit Berkley Square the roads were paved. Given the social conditions of our newly adopted town, the operators of the Moulin Rouge tried to make us as comfortable as possible by purchasing some of the newly built stucco homes for the entertainers and some of the staff. This is where I finally found Anna and several of the others. They were glad to see me and, of course, I was especially happy to see Anna. After sharing my stories about the trip and getting an update on the hotel, I collapsed into bed.

When I woke up the next morning, it was quiet. Everyone had already left for the Moulin Rouge to continue rehearsing and preparing for the hotel's opening. I was anxious to start the day with an inspection of the surrounding properties in this newly developed area within the shadow of the old shanties and dirt roads.

As I drove down "D" Street toward Bonanza, it was clear the opening of a hotel-casino in the area was sparking some excitement. I peered out the window at new businesses along the road, including local markets and motels like the Mo Mart and the West Motel, which were obviously hoping to piggyback onto the Rouge's customers and workers. The major investors, Lou Rubin, Will Max Schwartz, and Alexander Bisno, may have been on to something, I figured. They believed the time was right for an integrated casino in Las Vegas that would cater to blacks from more cosmopolitan cities such as Los Angeles, as well as whites who wanted to see some of the top black entertainers from around the world. It also gave visitors of color who weren't welcome to stay overnight on the Strip — including some of its showroom headliners and lounge acts — a place other than private boarding houses to rest their heads. In return, from what I could tell on that first look around, the hotel construction and influx of employees flocking into town had given rise to a new business community.

As I continued my drive, it wasn't long before I realized all these investments weren't just based on thin hopes. Heading west on Bonanza — the road of demarcation between the black and white areas of town — this elegant, bright, pale-yellow building appeared from nowhere, as if I had stumbled upon a jewel in the dust. Palm trees lined the exterior, where columns and signs were accented in red. My eyes were immediately drawn to the beautifully scripted words, "Moulin Rouge," that loomed above the hotel like a beacon. On the face of a rectangular spire that rose a couple of stories above the hotel were lighted signs advertising the name and an outline of the Eiffel Tower; perfect for the hotel's theme and, surely I thought, a head-turner for blocks around.

I walked inside and the place took my breath away. The carpeting was bright and colorful; it looked like you could sink into it. Polished mahogany paneling framed the walls, and above the bar an artist had painted a signature mural of African American dancing girls in colorful French costumes. Some of the furniture was covered in leather and velvet, and crystal chandeliers dipped down from the ceilings. My imagination went wild. I could see customers at the gaming tables, the band playing in the background, and the dealers saying, "Place your bets. Place your bets." No expense had been spared. It was as beautiful as anything I had seen in New York. And that included our corner of the enterprise: the Café Rouge showroom boasted about 500 seats, sophisticated lighting and sound equipment, and perhaps the most modern projection booth in the city.

I was suddenly brought back to reality when my producer, Clarence Robinson, walked over and greeted me with a hug. "Glad to see you," he said. "Rehearsals are going really well," he added, and started to bring me up to speed. The *Tropi-Can-Can* revue included show-stopping dance numbers like the Watusi, with its wild gyrations, and the thrilling cancan, which would introduce Las Vegas to the Parisian cabaret high kicks three years before the Stardust brought the actual *Lido de Paris* to town. There was one point in the Watusi when the girls had to jump up, hit the floor doing the splits, spin around and jump back up again, and it all had to be done at least six times in a row at a rapid-fire tempo. Anna and the other girls wore long green and yellow feathers that flowed down to the floor like a peacock's and form-fitting sequined bodices. There was a "Gabriel's horn" number when they came down some stairs dressed in white satin, like angels, and a fun Caribbean selection to the tune of "Two Ladies in de Shade of de Banana Tree" from Pearl Bailey's Broadway show *House of Flowers*. Of course, all the dancers were African American and every shade of gorgeous.

Clarence Robinson had directed shows at the original Moulin Rouge in Paris, and had been director of the London Palladium for several years. Benny Carter was a jazzman who had made a successful transition into arranging and scoring for movies. He had composed hits such as "Black Bay Boogie" and "Blues in My Heart," and a hotel press release printed in *the Las Vegas Sun* not long before the opening touted him as "America's most versatile bandleader," able to play trumpet, piano, saxophone, and clarinet.

The staff's dress fit the theme of the hotel perfectly. The dealers wore colorful French attire with arm quarters, and the cigarette girls had ruffled panties and French boutique hats. Men hired as hotel security were dressed in French policemen's uniforms and the waiters were fitted for tuxedos, with white shirts and bow ties.

Some of the staff had to be trained to work on the casino floor, because the only casino jobs for African Americans at that time were in the back of the house: the maids and janitorial porters. The owners of the Moulin Rouge hired a man named Pat Patterson, a highly touted maitre d' from the West Coast, to recruit waiters from around the country, and the call for dancers and showgirls had gone out across the U.S. as well, in letters, magazines, and newspaper advertisements.

If you took all the entertainers and staff into account, you had African Americans from all over the world taking part in what was to be the first interracial hotel-casino of this caliber or size in the country. With this foundation, and the eventual clientele that came to the hotel, it would be safe to say the Moulin Rouge was the most cosmopolitan establishment in the city at that time — across the tracks and under the bridge notwithstanding.

Heavyweight boxing champion Joe Louis traveled the country as a kind of goodwill ambassador for months before the hotel opened. It was only four years after he lost his final fight to Rocky Marciano, and Lewis still held the fascination of upper-class blacks. He also was the hotel's official greeter, receiving a small share of ownership in the new venture in return. That made him the only black to have any investment share in the whole venture. Former Globetrotter basketball star Sonny Boswell was brought in as general manager after having the same positions at The Pershing Hotel in Chicago and Los Angeles.

During that opening week, the marquee value of Benny Carter was enhanced by entertainers such as Ann Weldon, a singer who recorded for RCA Victor, and Stump and Stumpy, a comedy dance team well known from the chitlin' circuit that many say "inspired" the early work of Dean Martin and Jerry Lewis. There was also no shortage of entertainment for the lounge, which included the soon-to-be-famous Ahmad Jamal on piano.

During my two weeks of rehearsals for the show, I familiarized myself with the technical aspects such as the lighting and musical cues, the order of the acts, and came up with the banter I would use to make the transitions between the various numbers. My main job was to act as emcee, but I was also co-producer and sang during a few of the dance productions — up-tempo numbers such as "This is the Watusi" and "Blow Gabriel Blow." I also called time backstage every fifteen minutes to get the cast on their marks.

Everything was moving on schedule, but it wasn't until I saw the slot machines, craps tables, and roulette wheel brought into the building that I knew we were ready to take off. As opening night neared, you could feel the anticipation and excitement building. On the last day of rehearsals, we had a run-through with employees filling in as the audience. It was a free show and the complimentary drinks flowed, but their love of the robust *Tropi-Can-Can* was genuine.

On opening night, it seemed like every man or woman who was "somebody" in town showed up, including the mayor and administrators from the different hotels. I remember Tallulah Bankhead in the audience, along with Gary Cooper, Humphrey Bogart, and Joe Adams, a major radio personality from Los Angeles and film actor. There were also some folks flown in from New York by Louis Ruben, and reporters from some of the country's major black newspapers. It was an era in Vegas' colorful history that still embraced glamour, so the women came dressed in long gowns and cocktail dresses, while some of the men wore tuxedos. We even gave away silver dollars wrapped up in little velvet bags.

Some came to see the competition, some to pan the operation, and others to catch a red-hot "colored show." We gave them everything we had. A few days later Ralph Pearl of the *Las Vegas Sun* wrote that the "guys and gals in this super Clarence Robinson production out-Donn Arden and out-Ron Fletcher with their talents," referring to the two producer-choreographers who brought the

French showgirl look to the Strip. "They shake everything but the foundation, and on this I take an oath. Don't miss the Moulin Rouge food or the show."

We were officially a part of Las Vegas. Word got around and business began to pick up every night. Along with the customary shows at 8:15 and 11:15 PM, our public relations man Martin Black had the brilliant idea to try a third performance at 2:15 AM for the entertainers and musicians in town who were just getting off work, and the rounders who cruised from club to club all night. We tried it for a week, and discovered that was when the casino truly came to life. As time went on, the Moulin Rouge became a popular late-night — or should I say early-morning — hangout for everyone from chorus girls to major entertainers, who would take cabs and limos from the Strip. I never knew who I would see in the audience during the *Tropi-Can-Can*: Edward G. Robinson, Cary Grant, Sarah Vaughn, Tallulah Bankhead, Louis Armstrong, Frank Sinatra, Nat King Cole. And I can't think of a black entertainer who didn't, at some point, come over after a nightly gig on the Strip to hang out and have some fun.

After the shows we would gather in the lounge — singers, dancers, comedians, musicians, movie stars — to give impromptu performances. Sometimes it would turn into a blowout that lasted until the sun came up. One by one, performers such as Sammy Davis Jr., Lionel Hampton, singer Sonny King, and comedian George Kirby would get up to do their stuff in what we called cutting competitions, basically jostling one another to get time on stage. A comedian would start his jabs and before you knew it, somebody was shouting, "Sit down, you're not funny!" and the next hambone was up there. It was all just a free-for-all, with incredibly talented entertainers of every shade of skin.

In fact, probably the most amazing consequence of our opening was that blacks and whites could mingle together. When the Rouge opened, the casinos on the Strip took out the obligatory "Welcome to Town" ads, but it's my guess they figured the Rouge would be a convenient way to deflect black patrons away from places they weren't welcome. What they hadn't anticipated was that the Rouge would have the allure of forbidden fruit for white patrons. Nowhere else in town had that aura.

Showgirls from other productions were leaving the Strip after work and coming to our place, and where showgirls go, gamblers will follow. Casino managers started warning their girls that if they were caught pulling any of the players over to the Moulin Rouge, they would be fired. They even sent spotters to check on them, which slowed down our casino drop. But their players started hearing about the new restriction, and protesting that the girls be given special consideration. The first and foremost rule to a pit boss is, "Don't anger your players." They lifted the ban and the girls could once again be seen at our place.

Another plus was the casino's success being felt by the businesses, new and old, in the surrounding neighborhood. Moulin Rouge employees, unwelcome in the white sections of town, funneled their hard-earned wages and tips back into the local restaurants, stores, and clubs. These waiters, bartenders, waitresses, bellhops, and valets were a captured market, if you will, but they provided a welcome infusion of activity on the Westside. There was even talk of new hotels. The Carver House Hotel and Casino had been earmarked for the corner of "D" Street and Jackson Avenue, and a sign went up on empty land at the corner of Owens and "D" Street: "The Mardi Gras, Coming Soon."

Jackson Avenue had its own flavor and excitement. There were five blocks along the dirt road lined with casinos, restaurants, and nightclubs: the Wild West meets Bourbon Street. And it was jumping all the time. Men and women, black and white, would mill around with drinks in their hands, wandering from club to club; the fashionable Town Tavern, perhaps, or the rustic Brown Derby with its pine wood benches and elk horns on the walls. Cooks would baste their barbecued chicken and ribs in the windows to tempt us all inside. As the early morning sunlight finally poked its way through the swirling dust, you could hear the distant moan of a tenor sax or the soulful solo of a trumpet.

Musicians of every color would come to Jackson to play together: jazz, pop, blues. There was a sense of freedom along that avenue, in fact, that you didn't find anywhere else in Las Vegas and an undeniable harmony. The different races would intermingle, sharing their love of good music and good food, and there was this happiness because we were all simply enjoying one another's company without anyone telling us what we could or couldn't do. Jackson Avenue may have been born out of segregation, but it was sustained at that time by raw talent, a will to survive and a true feeling of independence.

The street usually came alive about 1 AM so we would head over after finishing up at the Rouge, hitting the El Morocco, the Cotton Club, occasionally even a private key club called the Key Club that had comfortable couches, and steaks and lamb chops on the menu. Sometimes after the sun came up, I would arrange to rent some horses and we would ride them up to the base of the surrounding mountain ranges. I can remember Nat King Cole and Sarah Vaughn on some of those rides. And it wasn't unusual to see at least one of us wearing cowboy attire, an extremely popular fashion choice in 1950s Las Vegas.

Of course, while the Moulin Rouge fed so much of the excitement and growth in the area, it wasn't invulnerable. Two performers died tragically during engagements at our hotel. One of them was the amazing tap dancer Teddy Hale, who died of a drug overdose. The other was Wardell Gray, a tremendously gifted tenor bebop saxophonist, whose body was found in the desert surrounding Las Vegas around the time of the hotel's opening. The cause of his death still remains a mystery, as there was never a full investigation. I hate to recall these memories, for both of the men were my friends. Sometimes you just don't know what people are into, even though you might see them every day.

As time wore on, and despite the fact that the shows were running smoothly and the place was a hit, there were rumors the casino was suffering cash flow problems. Anna and I didn't take any chances and started to watch our spending. We worked out a plan to live off of Anna's salary and save mine. In show business, you never know when the work is going to slow down, so you need that rainy-day fund. But we also knew it took a new establishment a while to get on its feet. There was always a shakedown period.

From the outside, in fact, everything looked fine. The cast was rehearsing new numbers. Name entertainers such as Lionel Hampton and Dinah Washington were brought in to retain the standing-room only crowds and keep new customers coming through the doors. Then the management brought in Les Brown and his Band of Renown. This was a significant step for, up until that time, we had an all-black cast and orchestra so we were looking forward to the first integrated show at the hotel. I remember the band's opening was star-studded and jam-packed. Afterward, we boogied until the wee hours of the morning, then went over to the Cotton Club on Jackson Avenue and partied some more. Everyone at the hotel was looking forward to a great four weeks with the band, but it wasn't in the cards.

Looking back, it was clear there was money going out the back door as fast as it was coming in the front door; somebody was stealing, though whether one of the investors was shafting the others was harder to know. The rumors started circulating about four months after the hotel opened that the lenders were getting extensions on their short-term debts and vendors would only deliver supplies "cash on delivery." We figured this was normal for a new business during the first few months. Then the unions representing the performers started demanding that labor bonds and contract obligations be in place in the event of closure. The Moulin Rouge also had several small stockholders, investors who put down about $10,000 each, who started to get worried. At one point, they came into town and demanded something be done to control the hemorrhaging.

It finally came crashing down in October. The last night began as usual, with everyone engrossed in their normal routines. The musicians tuned up while the technicians checked the lights and sound. The dancers and showgirls made last-minute inspections of their costumes and I was doing my vocal exercises backstage. The show was about to start when I got a phone call from the front of the house: "Hold the show until we get back to you."

This was odd, to say the least. The showroom was filling up, and a line of customers weaved from the entry door back toward the restaurant. Ten minutes passed. Fifteen. A half hour. We were all starting to panic. Finally, I received the devastating second phone call. There would be no show. The hotel was closing.

As an announcement was made to the audience, sheriff's deputies came into the casino and turned the slot machines so they faced the walls. They seized the chips on the tables, the drop boxes, and the money in the cage. Everything was in disarray, yet the sheriff's men knew exactly what they were doing. The bar and restaurant customers were allowed to finish their meals and drinks, but then had to leave the premises unless they were staying in the hotel.

The next few days were filled with remorse and confusion among all of us. It was as though we were at a wake — and to some extent it was. Talk had been circulating about a possible closure, but the amount of business coming in didn't seem to warrant such a reality.

Looking back, a combination of factors probably added up to that rapid demise. First, a lack of accounting that permitted some form of skim, with or without investor knowledge. Add to that the fact that 1955 would go down as one of Las Vegas' first boom-to-bust cycles of overbuilding. Three major hotels opened that year; the Riviera, Royal Nevada, and the Dunes, the latter debuting only a week before the Rouge. Though we had the most distinct product, there simply may not have been enough room for all of us. (The Royal Nevada also went belly-up, and was eventually annexed by the Stardust.)

Finally, the reason that went down in Las Vegas legend: There was undeniable pressure coming from the other casinos for our lenders to call in our short-term notes. In other words, we were a threat. Too successful for our own good. Of course, time went on to show Las Vegas casino operators they better get used to growth and competition. The next three years would bring the Hacienda, Tropicana, and Stardust, respectively.

The sudden closure created a rash of problems which come when you have a few hundred people thrown out of work, most of them away from home and in a segregated town where the only service-industry jobs for people of color are both menial and low-paying. (Beyond the Strip, blacks did sometimes fare better working in the industrial plants and at the Nevada Test Site.)

Lucky for the show personnel, the union had insisted upon that cash bond for a whole pay period. At least it would be enough to get everyone home. The housing, which had been supplied by the hotel, was also a part of the seizure and the employees were given two weeks to vacate. I will always remember how the business owners on Jackson Avenue came forward with a pool of money to help some of the stranded workers get home by bus. A few Westside owners also picked up Rouge employees to work in their stores and nightclubs.

It was a sad time for us, more than just the closing of another show and time to look for the next one. I believe if the Moulin Rouge had stayed open, the Westside would have kept growing. The hotel was the cornerstone for the whole area, and an excuse for folks of all kinds to congregate. There was nothing like it.

After the comet-like rise and fall of the hotel, you would think Anna and I would pack up and leave as soon as we could. We weren't allowed to choose where we lived, or where we shopped. Even if we had gotten jobs on the Strip right away, we wouldn't have been able to walk through the front door. Compared to New York, this town was full of dust and little promise.

But we did stay. I had found something in Las Vegas I had not found anywhere else — a glimmer of hope, you might say. Looking up!

Photo courtesy of William H. "Bob" Bailey

Bob Bailey at age sixteen.

Photo courtesy of Culturally Diverse Advertising

Bob Bailey

Photo courtesy of *Las Vegas Review-Journal*

Count Basie

Photo courtesy of Culturally Diverse Advertising

Billie Holiday

Photo courtesy of *Las Vegas Review-Journal*

Bailey and showgirls look at Moulin Rouge contract.

Photo courtesy of *Las Vegas Review-Journal*/Jeffrey McCillan

Dr. James McMillan, president of NAACP, at head of table, for a meeting on desegregation held at Moulin Rouge coffee shop in 1960. Also present (left to right) are: Hank Greenspun, Mayor Oran Gragson, Dr. Charles West, Police Chief Ray Schaeffer, and Donald Clark of NAACP.

Photo courtesy of Culturally Diverse Advertising

Anna Porter Bailey

Photo courtesy of Culturally Diverse Advertising

Pearl Bailey

Photo courtesy of Culturally Diverse Advertising

Louis Armstrong and Bob Bailey

Duke Ellington

Duke Ellington

Photos courtesy of *Las Vegas Review-Journal*/Sony Music/Josephine Mangiaracina

Ella Fitzgearld performs in Las Vegas.

Photos courtesy of *Las Vegas Review-Journal*

Photo courtesy of Culturally Diverse Advertising

Nat King Cole — later played on Bailey's TV show.

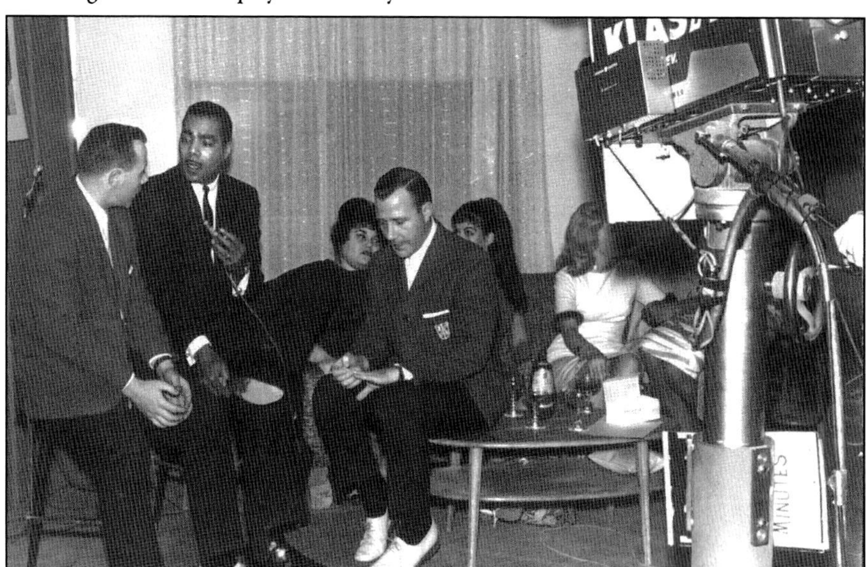

Photo courtesy of William H. "Bob" Bailey/Chet Krantz

Taping of *Twin Tunes* from the Channel 8 studio.

Photo courtesy of William H. "Bob" Bailey

Ed Sullivan, Sally Blair, and Bob Bailey.

Photo courtesy of William H. "Bob" Bailey

Martin Luther King Jr. visits Las Vegas. Back row: (unknown), Judge Robert Reid, Margie Elliott, Anna Bailey. Front row: Martin Luther King Jr., Bob Bailey, Jerry Spencer, Sandra Reid.

Photo courtesy of Culturally Diverse Advertising

Sammy Davis Jr., a regular visitor on Bailey's TV show when playing at the Sands Hotel.

Photos courtesy of *Las Vegas Review-Journal*/JC Kodey

Bailey plans national NEDCO procurement conference.

Photos courtesy of *Las Vegas Review-Journal*

Bill Cosby and Sidney Poitier with Bob Bailey, and George Foreman in *Let's Do It Again*.

Photo courtesy of William H. "Bob" Bailey

Bob Bailey presents an award to Elizabeth Dole, U.S. Secretary of Transportaion.

Photos courtesy of *Las Vegas Review-Journal*/JC Kodey

Senator Harry Reid (far right) worked alongside many local activists, including (left to right) Dr. Bob Bailey, Dr. James McMillan, and former Moulin Rouge co-owner, Sarann Knight-Preddy.

Photo courtesy of William H. "Bob" Bailey

Bailey receiving his Doctorate of Humane Letters.

Photos courtesy of *Las Vegas Review-Journal*

Moulin Rouge as it appeared in 1993.

Photo courtesy of William H. "Bob" Bailey

Bailey in his office.

Photo courtesy of William H. "Bob" Bailey

Bob Baily with General Collin Powell.

Photo courtesy of William H. "Bob" Bailey

Bailey reports on Middle East trade mission.

Photos courtesy of *Las Vegas Review-Journal*/Craig L. Moran

Gladys Knight at the Flamingo Hilton, performed in the Bob Bailey production, Vocal Extravaganza in Black TV special.

Photo courtesy of William H. "Bob" Bailey

Bob Bailey meets with Kuwaiti dignitaries on a groundbreaking Department of Commerce trip to introduce minority-owned businesses to the Middle East.

Photo courtesy of William H. "Bob" Bailey

Bailey with Governor Kenny Guinn and Bill Cosby.

Photo courtesy of William H. "Bob" Bailey

Bob Bailey with Dick Gregory

Photo courtesy of William H. "Bob" Bailey

Bailey and Andrew Young

Photos courtesy of *Las Vegas Review-Journal*/Shelly Donahue

Gerald Wilson, a Count Basie associate, conducts the UNLV Jazz Orchestra at a concert in Las Vegas.

Photo courtesy of William H. "Bob" Bailey

Dr. William H. "Bob" Bailey

Photo courtesy of William H. "Bob" Bailey

Anna and Bob Bailey

Photo courtesy of William H. "Bob" Bailey

Bob Bailey, Count Basie, and Sammy Davis, Jr. backstage at the Sands in the early 1980s.

Photo courtesy of William H. "Bob" Bailey

John Bailey, Bob and Anna Bailey at the deication of Dr. William H. "Bob" Bailey Middle School.

Photo by Shari Thomas

The Bailey Family in 2008.

Chapter 6

One Door at a Time

I think we were among the few who stayed. All the Moulin Rouge people thought we were crazy. But there was a big reason why I didn't want to leave: I had a TV show.

I had found something I was looking for that I couldn't find anywhere else. I had already tried in New York, Chicago, Detroit, and Miami, and none of those places would even hire me as a dolly pusher to guide the camera around the studio floor.

But then my break came. Midway through the Moulin Rouge's brief moment in the sun, I met Charles "Buck" West, the state's first black physician and the owner of a newspaper for the black community called the *Las Vegas Voice*. Anna and I hit it off with Buck, who would become our best friend. Buck introduced us to the editor of the *Voice*, a tenacious lady in her mid-forties named Alice Key — or, I should say, *reintroduced* one of us, because

Anna had briefly met her in the Bronx the night the club kept me waiting on the sidewalk during the party for her.

One day, we started brainstorming for ideas on how to get locals from beyond the Westside to come explore our food and entertainment. Alice mentioned how great it would be to have a television show featuring all the entertainers who came to town. Bells went off in my head like a jackpot on a dollar slot machine.

Martin Black, the Rouge's publicity director, said, "Bob, didn't you go to television school?"

I smiled. "I just happen to have a show in my bag." It was a scripted TV variety show, packaged and ready to go. My student project in New York also could serve as a tangible example of what we were pitching. Black quickly sold the idea to the Moulin Rouge management. Now I had a show *and* a sponsor. The next step would be the most difficult. What chance did a black TV show have of getting on the air in a town as highly segregated and discriminatory as Las Vegas? I decided I had been turned down so many times, one more wouldn't phase me. Besides, I had gotten one step further than I ever had before: I had a sponsor. 'Here we go!' I thought. 'Here we go!'

We set up an appointment with Hank Greenspun, the *Las Vegas Sun* newspaper publisher who also owned KLAS-TV Channel 8, the city's first and only television station at the time. I was nervous, but Alice and Martin were ready to chime in to confirm the Rouge's support and talk about all the new viewers the show could attract.

When we finished our pitch, I asked, anxiously, "What do you think?"

"When do you want to start?" Hank said.

He then called in his station manager and program director, and asked them to help us in whatever way necessary.

I think we caught Hank at a good time. He was looking for variety for his programming and we offered something totally different, along with a new potential market. You can depend on the do-gooder attitude to get you so far, and Hank was certainly known for that. But it helps if the do-gooder is going to make some money too.

Hank knew he would catch a lot of hell; racist comments and telephone calls. It didn't take long. The calls started coming right after the promotions aired and print ads proclaimed, "Las Vegas makes history [with] first all-Negro TV show." But we moved ahead, undaunted and indifferent. If Hank was going to stand up for us, we would give him the best we had.

It seems as if everyone who had a TV set tuned in for the debut of *Talk of the Town*. I directed and Alice and I worked together as co-hosts. Alice, who was very fair, wore darker makeup so she would look a little more like me. I didn't want to scare the bigots into thinking I was sharing a soundstage with a white woman. I couldn't forget that warehouse encounter in Atlanta.

That first program was primitive, like everything in the early days of television. Nothing was pre-recorded, everything was live; the camera would rest on a title card while we changed scenes. It was prohibitively expensive to try to record any of our work, so nothing from those early days survives. But what a moment in time those shows would be to see entertainers from the Moulin Rouge and later, the Strip, singing with our trio on the variety show.

The show was a hit. Some of the smaller sponsors threatened to pull their ads, but Hank just smiled and said, "Let them go to another TV station." (Remember, Channel 8 was the only game in town.) I think he was pleasantly surprised at what a class show it was, and he took me under his wing as a mentor after hearing how hard it was to break into media elsewhere. As the show progressed during the next several weeks, we gave the hotels great exposure by bringing in their performers, working closely with their public relations departments.

And I was on cloud nine. I still couldn't believe I had a TV show in the "Mississippi of the West" after being turned down by all of the liberal stations in the East and Midwest. One thing this experience taught was that you never know when or where your opportunity will present itself. Just make sure you're ready when it comes your way.

BUT NOW THE ROUGE, THE PRIMARY SPONSOR, was gone. Still, I decided to stay if I could find a way to keep the TV show on the air. I was beginning to feel some investment in the community. Dr. Mays of Morehouse College had always preached the notion of sharing your success, of giving something back to your people. As I looked around and talked to some of the old-timers, it became clear there was enough work to do for a lifetime. By having a presence on TV, by crossing that barrier, I started to realize this was a town where I could make a difference. God knows, Las Vegas was certainly in need of support, leadership, and community development.

The only thing we had to figure out was how to pay for the TV show. The Moulin Rouge had financed all the episodes we had done so far, and stood as the major sponsor for the entire 13-week contract. "Go ahead, see if you can find other sponsors," Hank told me. Alice became our saleswoman, talking black business owners along Jackson Avenue into buying ad time. We even managed to attract some interest from sponsors beyond the black area who saw the potential of the show.

So here was everything I had been looking for: my own television show, a chance to improve the black community, and a sweetheart. Why would I leave? Where else would I go?

Well, at least I had a sweetheart somewhere. "I thought Las Vegas was the worst place in the world," Anna says now. "What do we want to stay here for?" she asked. "We can't go downtown to eat without getting food to go and eating it on the sidewalk." So, we agreed it wouldn't threaten our marriage for her to go back out on the road. Anna auditioned for shows in Los Angeles but just couldn't crack the market. So she signed up with producer Larry Steele, whose traveling road show had been part of our friendly competition in those Atlantic City summers.

To fully understand our separation, it's time to confess another detail. Most of the ad revenue generated by the TV show was going right to the station; I was basically doing it gratis in return for the opportunity, considering it my "rehearsal hall," to be ready when the call came from some larger city. At some point, Alice had to get back to

Los Angeles, so I had to take on the sales job as well. You can imagine what a relief it was to get a call from Jimmy Gay, one of the black movers and shakers in town: "Hey Bob, how would you like to be on the radio?"

Radio station KENO had asked Jimmy to do a black-oriented shift as a dee-jay. But he recommended me, given my momentum with the TV show and past training at television and radio school.

When I went in for the interview, the station manager assumed he would have to put me on a shift when a technician was there to work the board for me. When I told him I already had a broadcast license and could work my own board, I was hired on the spot. Now I not only had a TV show, but a radio show — and this one paid! You never know when your opportunity is coming. Just make sure you're ready to meet it head on. In afternoon shifts, I would play the rock 'n' roll hits of the day, Little Richard and the like, for the kids. The night shift brought more Sinatra and jazz or blues standards. Unlike today's formatted radio stations, the KENO dee-jays determined the format for their shift. I came right on after a country personality known as Pappy, who would announce his dislike for my musical choices with a dog howl from his canine "sidekick."

Las Vegas was still a very strange place, so exciting and unique, yet so backward at the same time. My TV and radio jobs now entitled me to join the small press corps of those invited to cover the opening nights of new casino headliners, many of whom I would later interview on the air. That would often make me, very conspicuously, the only black person in the audience (or one of two, when

Anna was in town). Occasionally, invitations went out to Jimmy or to the black community leaders, Buck West and James McMillan, the first black doctor and dentist in the state. Anna remembers sitting at the same table as Bob Hope at one of the shows. "He was sitting a little bit in front of us," she remembers, "and he kept turning around looking. I guess he wanted to see if we were somebody."

Of all the black entertainers who worked Las Vegas in the segregated era, Josephine Baker generated the most excitement. The celebrated American dancer had moved to Paris in the 1930s and was now synonymous with the sophistication of more open-minded Europe. But dusty Las Vegas was abuzz when she came to play the El Rancho Vegas. Local dignitaries greeted her at the airport and her first show drew a standing ovation. When she retired to her dressing room, however, she was dismayed. Why had none of her people come out to see her? When she mentioned that to her dresser, she was clued in that blacks were not allowed in the customer areas of the hotel. Baker was relieved that there was a reason why no blacks were in the audience, but angry about the reason. She summoned hotel owner Beldon Katleman to her dressing room. She was direct and straight to the point: "If I don't see some black faces in the audience for my second show, there will not be another show."

I got a call at the radio station. Katleman was audibly upset and needed some quick advice on how to pull in some black people and fast. I said it would take too long to line up a sufficient number of my friends. "Why don't you do this?" I suggested. "Tell some of your maids and porters to run home and get dressed in their best clothes and get back in time for the second show."

It worked. Baker performed, and for the rest of the run, it was required to have at least one table, preferably two, set aside for black people. By the way, their dinners were free too.

The black entertainers did my TV show, so almost by default, I ended up being their host around town. It was great to make these contacts that sometimes grew into friendships, but also disparaging. Several times I had to ask myself again, 'What are you doing here?' I wonder how long I would have stuck it out if I had not been accepted in the media.

Hank Greenspun sold Channel 8, but I was given a great offer at Channel 13, the second station to open in town (my, how Vegas was growing). Channel 13's studio was located in the Fremont Hotel in the heart of downtown's famous "Glitter Gulch." Remember, the Strip was segregated more in deference to the gamblers who came from racist states. But some of the key operators, like Jack Entratter at the Sands, were worldly Easterners; Entratter had managed New York's famed Copacabana club and was a fair-minded person. Whenever I wanted to go to the Sands, I would call him and he would give an OK from the doorman all the way through the "check points" to let me in.

But downtown? It was proudly Western, or redneck, if you prefer. The "sawdust joints" still sported Western saloon motifs and now remained as a choice for those who preferred the World War II, pre-Sands era of Vegas to the "carpet joints." Prior to my arrival, there had been trouble between rednecks and black airmen from Nellis Air Force Base, so downtown was officially declared "off limits" to them, and unofficially to everybody else.

Hence, the reaction of the Fremont Hotel security guard I described in the introduction. He followed me in and followed me out every day for about two weeks. After a week or so, I made a coded, tongue-in-cheek mention on one of my broadcasts about all the "protection" I had on property. A week or so after that, Alex Gold, the station manager, was visibly disturbed to pass along the hotel manager's request that I use the back door. He was Jewish, he explained, and had endured hate and discrimination as a young man coming up in Georgia. So there I was, a TV host with a boss who could sympathize, but neither of these things good enough to let me walk through the front door.

That gave me just a little taste of how it was to be someone like Nat King Cole. One night when Nat was performing at the Sands, I tagged along with him and Al Freeman, the Sands' publicity director, as they headed to the Tropicana. Nat wanted to say hello to an old friend who was appearing there, fellow performer Arthur Lee Simpkins. But we were abruptly stopped at the front door by security and reminded that blacks were not welcome in the hotel.

"Don't you know who this is? This is Nat King Cole," Freeman protested.

"I don't care if he is the black Jesus. He can't come in," the guard snapped. Al was about to deck him, but Nat cooled him down. "I'm just doing my job," the guard said. He suggested we go to the stage door and not through the lobby. Al had a better idea: "Screw this place. We'll go the Sahara and see Louis Prima instead."

So off we went. (It didn't take long to cover those three miles of Strip like it does now.) It looked like this was going to go better. The valet greeted us, recognizing Nat and even me from my TV show. He wouldn't have seen me there before; other than press nights when I was a guest, I always went through the stage door with my cameraman. But as we approached the front door, here came security. My heart was beating fast. Standing in the doorway, the guard explained that he knew who Nat was, but his orders were to tell all black persons they were not welcomed.

Al was livid by now and demanded he see his counterpart, a PR director who had been forewarned we were coming to the lounge show. By now, more security had gathered around to see what the problem was. While all this was going on, people started approaching Nat to get his autograph. The first security guard was getting more and more embarrassed, and encouraged us to wait for someone to come give him the OK to let Nat in. But by now, Nat had had it. "Let's go back to the Sands, where I can go through the front door," he said.

I WAS STILL TRYING TO FIGURE OUT HOW TO get myself through another front door: The one at the Fremont. There was some public indignation from my co-workers about this whole treatment. One day, I was called into the accounts office. Flora Dungun was the financial officer and an outspoken women's rights activist, not to mention a civil rights advocate. "Do you have plans for lunch? . . . Would you care to join me?"

I hesitated but agreed. If she wanted to take the chance, I wouldn't be the one to chicken out, even though I had never been in the one-on-one company of a white woman in Las Vegas. "Where are we going?" I asked.

Without missing a step, she answered, "The coffee shop."

"Here?"

"Of course." We stopped for a minute to debate the pros and cons. This wasn't just one battle. It was as "unacceptable" for me to be in the coffee shop as to be seen in public with a white woman. But she was so insistent that finally I said, "The hell with it. Let's do it."

I carried my briefcase to reinforce that this was a business lunch. When the hostess saw us walking up, she abruptly turned and walked away as if she were attending to some other matter. We stood there with egg on our faces. Customers started to glance up at us. The hostess came back, but still managed to ignore us while seating a couple of people who had walked up behind us. Finally, when the hostess walked away again, Flora said, "I've waited long enough. There's a table. Let's sit down."

All eyes were on us but nobody moved or got up to leave. I could tell the hostess didn't know what, if anything, to do about us taking the table. After the initial shock, the customers quit staring, but no waitress came to take our order. We realized that while no security guards had come to confront us, we were simply being ignored in hopes that we would go away. I was embarrassed and thought about getting up to leave, but then decided that I was in so deep now, I was going to have to see it through. A half hour went by. Flora was burning, angrier than I. Here was someone facing discrimination for the first time, someone who wouldn't normally be in this position. She told me to wait and disappeared. A few minutes later she came back with a gentlemen I later found out was the pit boss. He talked to the hostess, who finally sent the waitress over. Later, the hostess dropped by our table and explained, as so many people had in this town, that she was "just following orders."

The next day, all hell broke loose. The hotel manager called Flora and they all went to meet with Alex, the station manager. I think the pit boss was called into it, too. Later in the day, I was called to the station an hour before my show. My first thought? "They're going to cancel my show." It was a little television personality going up against a big Las Vegas casino, and everyone knew who was going to lose.

When I got there, Alex and Flora looked at me with stern faces that lit up with smiles as they announced the news. "Guess what, Bob? You don't have to come in through the servants' entrance anymore." Moreover, I could feel free to frequent any hotel facilities except the games themselves. (That didn't bother me; I got gambling out of my system during the Basie days.) I was elated. We won a battle without going through any protests, such as bringing in the NAACP.

THE NAACP WAS PLENTY BUSY NONETHELESS. The Moulin Rouge didn't last long as a casino, but it brought a new surge of black energy to Las Vegas. During the next four years, the NAACP started lighting a fire under the state legislators to pass a civil rights law in Nevada. The first goal was access to public accommodations; equal opportunities in employment and banking would come later. Early leaders of the organization were honest and forthright, but they were working-class people who depended on the white system for their paychecks. Buck West, the family doctor, had moved to Las Vegas in 1954. He was out of the Washington tier of upper-class blacks, a third-generation doctor well known in the cultural circles of New York, Chicago, and California. For a while, Dr. West was the only person who had a phone north of Jackson Avenue. The dentist James McMillan was a friend of West. The doctor stored and warehoused his dental equipment while McMillan served in the military. During a weekend visit, McMillan was impressed by the Las Vegas weather compared to Detroit. What impressed him more was helping out a Moulin Rouge casino guest with a minor dental problem and being paid in casino chips worth $100. Both men were successful professionals, but they still felt the indignity that gnaws at you when you're the target of a segregated society.

The two doctors were qualified and independent, and stepped up to the leadership roles that were natural, given their status and the fact that nobody could cut their money off; it was derived from the black community itself. McMillan was chosen to run for president of the NAACP and West would head the Voters League, the nonpartisan political arm of the movement. Both doctors had relationships with the culinary union, which had seventy to eighty percent black membership with its maids, porters, and kitchen help. My job was to handle the publicity, and serve as press and event coordinator.

My radio and TV shows both were moving right along. By now I was doing my radio show on a remote hookup from a record shop called Larry's Music Bar on Jackson Avenue. Five days per week I would broadcast from 4 to 6 PM and literally stop traffic. When I would say, "Drive by and honk your horn," traffic would back up on that dusty, still-unpaved road, and the police would have to tell drivers to keep moving. We would get calls from other parts of town, and students from Las Vegas High would come over with their black student friends. Segregation laws and customs have never been able to keep people apart when they want to be together.On the Strip, however, economics — mainly the protests of big players from the South — still clipped off any small attempts to test the segregation policy. We didn't seem to be asking for much: The ability to go in and out of any place that has a public license, which is essentially a part of our rights as citizens.

Things were moving in the right direction, but the wolves were out. McMillan was drawing new membership to the NAACP, which focused on strategies for eliminating discriminatory policies. West was building the political machine with the Voters League, which focused on candidates and voter registration. It was crucial for these two forces to work in tandem and fend off the old "divide and conquer" tricks. In the initial stages of the civil rights initiative, the two doctors would be invited together to meetings with politicians or casino owners. Now the civic and business officials were beginning to invite them separately, a clear attempt to fracture the solidarity of the two organizations.

I was close to both, and aware of what the outside forces were trying to do. I compared notes with the two doctors, pushing these private invitations into the open and reinforcing our solidarity. "Take this as a warning," I advised them. "These tactics will be tried again and again if they sense a crack in the constituency." The movement was gaining strength and the old leadership was gathering around the new to make it stronger than ever.

Little did I know that show business was about to pull me away from the fight.

WHILE I WAS GETTING MORE FULLY IMMERSED in Las Vegas and learning who pulled the strings, Anna continued to travel. Her tours with Larry Steele's *Smart Affairs* had given way to more and more work with Pearl Bailey, four years of it. I got to see a little more of Anna when she worked for Pearlie Mae, because Pearl was a frequent and popular headliner on the Strip, having broken through any resistance there while I was still in school. Pearl was a champion of Las Vegas, and long before we got the Moulin Rouge job would tell Anna and me, "Las Vegas is where you have to go. That's where it's happening."

But during one show at the Flamingo, Pearl fell and injured herself. Did it stop her? Hell, no. She just rolled out onstage in a wheelchair the next night and broke everyone up. But on the engagement's closing night, she asked Anna if I would come down to the dressing room and meet with her. 'She wants me to be her opening act!' I thought. It made perfect sense as a way to reduce her stage time until she could get around better.

I started vocalizing to get my singing voice back into shape and even began thinking about a reasonable salary range. With a sharp outfit and a positive attitude, I headed to the Flamingo, caught the last show and went backstage for the closing-night party. As the party thinned, she beckoned me into the dressing room: "Come talk to me, Cuz." (We called each other cousins, but we never followed the bloodlines to figure out if we were really related.)

She started out as I had anticipated: "I have this tour signed for a whole year, but I can't do everything I usually do from this wheelchair . . ." she said. Wait, here it comes!

"I want you to come on board as my road manager."

Road manager?

"I know you did a good job for Clarence Robinson, and it would let you and Anna be together more often."

After I regained my composure, I asked for a night to think about it. If she had really wanted my singing act, I would have agreed on the spot. But weighing the merits of a road manager's gig against my TV show and community involvement, well that was a serious decision. And there was Anna — we would either be apart for another year unless she quit the show. We finally decided the tour could be a positive move. I had established myself in the media here, and thought it would not be hard to reestablish myself after my return. Traveling with Pearl might open up some new doors, plus we would be back to the business of saving one income and living off the other.

And my community activism? The civil rights crusade was a concern. But as my mother used to say when someone would have to drop out of a family effort, "One monkey never stops the show."

Two weeks later I was in New York, immersed in learning the duties of payroll, contracts with venues, transportation for people and props, checking hotel accommodations for the girls, dressing room assignments, lighting and sound cues, and getting paid by promoters. On top of all this, I had to send in a weekly income-and-expense report to the New York office. It was a lot to absorb, but after the first month or so it became mostly routine.

My most important job was to see to it that Pearl didn't have to worry about the business of the show and its movement. She was a little cranky on the first few engagements in the wheelchair. I was glad when she was back on her feet. So was her husband, the tremendous drummer, Louie Bellson. He used to get chewed out royally, but he would take it with a smile on his face. The road was tough, but some of the breaks were fun. Rehearsals would sometimes be on Pearl's ranch in Victorville, California; perfect for relaxing, horseback riding and good vittles. We were all glad to see Pearl go to the ranch during a break, as she came back in a good mood.

She could be pretty rough when audience turnout was less than expected, or when a show was canceled for some reason or another. Sometimes when she was distressed, she would call cast meetings and get on everybody's case. One of the worst times was when her tap-dancing brother, Bill Bailey, was late to one show and missed another one.

Instead of talking to Bill privately, she called a meeting. After she took on the girls, she lit into her brother. 'Doesn't she know he is on drugs?' I wondered. They went back and forth. I tried to stop the public scene and was told in no uncertain terms, "You stay out of it. This is a brother and sister affair." Bill finished the date, but was fired from the rest of the tour.

Pearl also had a good, warm side. Anna and I got paid even when we were on break or only working one or two days of the week. Once, she asked if I would drive her car from New York to Victorville. She proposed to make it a vacation for Anna and me. She flew us back to New York first-class, loading us up with a packet full of money and credit cards. She even suggested the best hotels to stay at along the way, and paid for them. Most of the dancers didn't know it, but Pearl paid their salaries out of her own pocket. The contracts were for her alone, and she could have toured lightly with a small band. But she wanted to provide work for the girls and the variety acts that made it a full show. I'm sure that on some of those soft financial weeks, she had to go into her personal salary to make payroll. Pearl was a real trouper.

As the tour was drawing to a close, we learned something else was going to change our lives: The impending arrival of a baby boy. It was time to get off the road and back to my TV and radio, so Anna could stay home with the baby.

❧

THANKFULLY, IT WAS AS EASY AS I HAD HOPED it would be to get back in full swing with the KLAS TV show and radio show on KENO. Community work was becoming very demanding as well. But on the battle front of our civil rights crusade, my suspicions had proved true: All the jostling for leadership in the movement was threatening the solidarity of the effort. It was clear that I quickly had to jump back into a role as medium between the doctors, West and McMillan. We needed a catalyst that would unite the total muscle of the various organizations and the churches. In lieu of civil rights legislation, the best choice seemed to be to push for a public policy of the state, because we had an ally in new governor Grant Sawyer.

Sawyer, a Nevadan since childhood, had grown up poor and gone on to law school, pursuing what he felt was a natural destiny to be a political leader. His mother was their small-town conscience in her efforts to help the unfortunate, "a raving radical," as he once called her. Sawyer built a reputation as a district attorney in Elko, eventually becoming state Democratic party chairman and organizing enough support to be seen as a viable candidate to run against the state's political machine in 1958.

Using the campaign slogan "Nevada Is Not For Sale," Sawyer pulled an upset in the primary election, thanks in part to the help of John F. Kennedy, who looked to Nevada as a state that could help him with his own presidential future. When Sawyer moved into the general election against two-term Republican Charles Russell, I changed parties. Remember, there was a time in this country when most African Americans were Republicans, the party of Lincoln who freed the slaves. But Sawyer really worked to establish a relationship with the black community.

I think I met Mr. Sawyer through Dr. West, when a number of us were invited to an open house to meet the candidate. Sawyer was on the same page as Kennedy in espousing civil rights, and he really impressed me as an individual with the acceptance he showed for the advancement of the social agenda and public desegregation. I was invited to join his support group and campaign for him, and didn't have to think very hard about switching parties.

I did a little bit of everything, working as a liaison between the campaign committee and the Voters League. I made a good conduit between the Sawyer campaign and the black community because, while I wasn't one of the official black leaders, I was the most visible black personality in Las Vegas, thanks to the TV and radio shows. I did a lot of outreach, a lot of PR work and a whole lot of walking for his election. But the black support became just part of a Democratic wave that included even the casinos deserting Russell; Sawyer won the governor's race by a record margin of 17,000 votes.

Once Sawyer took his oath of office in January 1959, the state was on our side. However, northern Nevada and the state capitol in Carson City held a general uneasiness about the casino climate in general, and the "silent ownership" — as in organized crime interests — of the southern Nevada casinos. And there was still no committed movement for change from the hotels and the general structure of the town. Frustration and anxiety were building in the Westside. People throughout the country were marching against injustice and segregation, while we were still holding meetings with no tangible results. The governor was on our side, but we felt that things were moving too slowly and we were going to take action as a community ourselves.

At one of our meetings, I suggested we must do something dramatic; otherwise we would only get more talk and little action. Las Vegas was such a hotspot, with the Rat Pack capturing the attention of Senator Kennedy and the rest of the nation during the filming of *Ocean's Eleven* in January 1960. It seemed like every third picture going out over the wire services was about Las Vegas. How do we play into that energy? McMillan proposed a march on the Strip. The timing would be perfect as a major boxing event was coming up and a full battery of the national press would be in town. Now was the time to make a move.

I was given the go ahead to get the PR moving. I called the Las Vegas News Bureau, the publicity arm of the Las Vegas Chamber of Commerce vested with keeping Las Vegas in the news. I sent a press release to the *Review-Journal* newspaper and made a personal call to Hank Greenspun at the rival *Sun*. All TV, radio, and newspapers broke the news at the same time: "NAACP plans march on the Strip."

Once the news of our "peaceful but firm demonstration" spread beyond the city limits, people began to cancel their room reservations. Our game strategy was to slow down tourism, and it was having immediate results. Who wanted a front-row seat to an ugly confrontation? The hotels launched a counteraction, threatening the maids and porters to bring pressure on the NAACP if they wanted to keep their jobs. The sheriff announced that he would be ready to combat any violence. In order to stay within the law, we went downtown to the county to get a permit. The only one they had on the books was a parade permit. We told them this would be a parade — a parade against ignorance and prejudice. Our music would be a loud speaker to lead the choir of marchers.

The atmosphere was getting strained and pressure was coming from every corner of the community. Pastors of the major churches began to question the wisdom of the march. The culinary union advised against it. Desert Inn boss Moe Dalitz used Sammy Davis Jr. as a middle-man to come ask me what it was we wanted, and whether I would be willing to meet with him. I agreed, but the call never came. Word even started to spread that the mob would put out a hit on McMillan if he didn't pull back. The casino bosses didn't need any spotlight on their activities; the only attention they wanted was on showgirls and Hollywood movie stars. They couldn't stand an investigation. We set up security measures to protect McMillan. The greater the effort to split the community and cancel the march, the closer West and McMillan came together and stayed the course as we neared the target date of March 26, 1960.

One of the ministers, Donald Clark, and David Hoggard, one of the NAACP's local heavyweights, played a strong role in keeping the marchers committed. We had hoped to have about three hundred people, a number that came into question when the casinos announced they would photograph all the marchers. Legitimately concerned about how many would show up, we publicized the fact that we had asked the national NAACP for help if there turned out to be mass arrests by the police. And to counter the threat of mob involvement or local casino employees being singled out for retaliation, we let word "leak" that blacks from larger cities would be coming in to join our march.

With all these threats and misinformation coming to a crescendo, Hank Greenspun called. "Can I set up a meeting to discuss what it would take to call off this march?"

I consulted the others and called him back. "We will be happy to meet," I told him, "as long as the governor is there." Sawyer's presence was needed to give the meeting the required authority, and any decisions that came of it would carry the clear message that the casino-supported candidate was part of it. The governor was fully aware of the march, but had so far opted to stay at a distance. Now he was willing to attend, but he was in New York and couldn't get to Las Vegas until the morning of the march.

On the morning of the 26th, Sawyer's assistant Dick Hamm and I were in the car that greeted the governor's plane at the airport. We headed to the Moulin Rouge, which had never regained its casino license but was open again as a bar and restaurant. All parties involved in the meeting agreed it would be "neutral territory," rather than asking the white officials to come down to Jackson Avenue, where the atmosphere was palpably hostile. As the car headed up the Strip, I briefed the governor, trying to distill the issues as simply as I could.

We had decided to go into the meeting asking for two key goals: Public accommodations in the casino, and jobs in middle management and gaming. The first had to be granted immediately; the rest could be hammered out in detail later. "We put together the march in order to display outwardly and for the press the segregated patterns in Las Vegas and the fact that they had to stop," I told him. "We no longer will accept the segregated policies the city is involved with."

We pulled into the Moulin Rouge right in time for the 8 AM meeting. I sat down at a long rectangular table with the governor and ten other men, including the Sheriff, "Butch" Leypoldt, and Clark County commissioners Art Olsen and Clesse Turner. Reporters listened from the other side of the room. Hank Greenspun started out by reminding everybody of the negative publicity this action would bring to the city; that photos of marchers in front of iconic neon marquees such as those at the Sands and Stardust would be burned into the minds of potential visitors. Dr. McMillan recapped our conditions: one, open the hotel accommodations to persons of color; two, employ dealers, cocktail waitresses, bartenders, waiters, security, desk clerks and hosts of color. Moreover, McMillan told the group that the general managers of the Desert Inn, Stardust, and Tropicana already had agreed in principle to open their facilities. Although we were all here at the table, the marchers were still on track to gather at the convention center later that day unless they received word from the committee not to.

Hank asked for a break in the meeting so he could make some telephone calls. He left the room and in less than half an hour, came back and called the meeting to order once again. I held my breath as he announced the casino owners had agreed to open public accommodations. Moreover, they agreed to meet during the week to discuss creating jobs for front desk clerks, bellhops, and valet parkers. It was all done in a half hour and a few phone calls!

A feeling of success and relief swept through our camp. We made it clear that the march was being "set aside," but not canceled until there was a clear indication the commitment was real and an employment plan would be produced within ninety days. Some of the black leaders were disappointed that we didn't push for more, and asked if the casino owners were yielding enough to suspend the march. Most angry was Ruby Duncan, president of the Welfare Women's Rights organization. But West and McMillan said, "We can always march if they don't do what they say they're going to do." And that's what they did.

And we understood Fremont Street would not be immediately included. Las Vegas mayor Oran Gragson was part of the meeting, and said that while he could not speak for the downtown businesses, the majority had agreed to further meetings toward the goal of expunging segregated policies. Despite these qualifications it was, as Dr. McMillan declared to the press, "a red-letter day in Las Vegas." Sawyer, Gragson, and the commissioners agreed to pursue the creation of a bi-racial civil rights commission.

THIS WAS A MAJOR VICTORY, BUT LARGELY A symbolic one at first. Maybe eighty percent of the hotels opened up, or made an attempt at public accommodation, but they made it so uncomfortable that it didn't encourage that much activity. Plus, a commitment could be retracted if management or ownership changed. The NAACP in Reno was watching our activity in Las Vegas. Eddie Scott came down from Reno to see how we had put our program together. If Reno would not open up to the black tourist, they, too, would be ready to march. What we needed now was a law on the books that would restrict segregation as a practice and pattern in the state of Nevada.

This pursuit had to be led by a person of stature, commitment, and political clout. Governor Sawyer was the natural choice, and he accepted the challenge. The next step was to get something started on a statewide basis that would outlaw discrimination with some sort of punitive recourse if the law was broken. We were all in agreement: You can't legislate a man's heart, but you can legislate his behavior.

In his 1960 state of the state address, Sawyer had strongly stated his position on guaranteeing equal rights to all Nevada citizens. He pushed for a law in his first legislative session, but his bill never left the Senate committee. However, Maude Frazier, a tough no-nonsense legislator introduced bill AB122, which provided for equal access to public employment opportunities as well as procurement projects using tax dollars. The weakness of the bill was that it didn't address the private sector, where the real action was. But this bill started the legislative movement in the right direction. AB122 passed both houses and was sent to the governor, who responded, "This is the first crack in the wall of discrimination in Nevada."

The next year, 1961, was supposed to bring the wall down altogether with the creation of the Nevada Commission on Equal Rights. The state legislature authorized the commission "to protect the welfare, prosperity, health and peace of all the people of the state, and to foster the right of all persons to reasonably seek, obtain and hold employment and housing accommodations, and reasonably to seek and be granted services in places of public accommodation without discrimination, distinction or restriction because of race, religious, creed, color, national origin or ancestry."

The commission didn't get any money, but it was given the right to do its own investigations and hold hearings, public or private. Its most important power was the ability to issue subpoenas if necessary. (And as it turned out, almost all of the gaming representatives had to be subpoenaed.) The information would be collected in a report for the governor and legislature, containing recommendations for future civil rights legislation. It was the first real legal tool we had to work with to expose the reality and depth of discrimination in Nevada. Our goals were to try and bring in the responsible people, the licensees, to tell us exactly what the policies of their hotels were. We thought we might get the state to come down on them if they weren't following its public policy. We would argue that if they weren't, they shouldn't be licensed by another state arm, the gaming control board.

Now it was time to go to work. Sawyer asked me if I would head the five-man commission; the first chairman had resigned. As the only minority member, I knew the importance of the task at hand better than anyone. You can talk about segregation and discrimination, but you don't really know how it really demeans an individual until you have actually experienced it. The governor had put himself on a political limb when he stood up to oppose segregation. I could do no less.

We established a format for the hearings, and decided to hold the first one in Reno in November 1962. I wrote opening remarks to use at all the meetings, setting the tone and atmosphere. We heard testimonies from the hotels, law enforcement, and state and local government officials. Most of it just documented what people already knew: Minorities in general, and African Americans in particular, were not allowed in the casinos, hotels, restaurants or other places of public accommodation. The employment picture was just as obvious. Blacks held no jobs other than those of maid or porters who swept the floors or cleaned bathrooms.

The picture was just as dismal in the government sector. Managers usually cited a lack of applicants, which minorities who attended the meetings refuted. One casino owner just flat out said he would not admit or hire "Negroes" unless the law required it. This testimony went on for two days. From time to time I had to call for a recess, as the audience got a little heated. I knew being on this body was going to be trying, but chairing it was even more of a challenge. Just as McMillan had received threats when he led the march campaign, I had received some seriously threatening calls. I would answer the phone to hear, "If you don't want to find yourself in a grave tomorrow, you better stop all this nonsense with these subpoenas." Click.

A couple of times, I had been tempted to join the movement of Martin Luther King, my friend from Morehouse days. But he would tell me, "Do what you have to do in Nevada. I'll take care of this." So here I was, doing it. And as chairman and the only person of color heading this effort, I stuck out like a sore thumb. Honestly, I had serious moments of apprehension during these hearings. But I tried to stay impartial and focus on getting the job done, and not let personal opinions get in the way.

And boy, did I have some opinions. The only reason there was a hotel room waiting in Reno was because the governor's office had set it up. Sometimes, during the testimony, my mind would float away. What a joke this was! Everyone in the state knew the policies, but we had to get people to go on the record. And the statistics were lining up very clearly to show disparity at every level.

The next stop was Hawthorne, and a hearing that came after my discovery the night before — you might recall if you started this book with the introduction —that the El Capitan, the city's crown jewel and major casino operation, would not let me stay there. Moreover, Gordon and Lindsay Smith, the owners of the El Capitan, had challenged our right to subpoena. They took us to court and filed injunctions for eight months. They refused to be told what they could or could not do.

I was up bright and early, happy to check out of the seedy motel I finally had found the night before. It was a one-day hearing in a town small by number, but significant because of the government installations, the Navy Ammunition Depot. The depot and the El Capitan accounted for most of the local economy. All of the support merchants — the grocery stores, gas stations, etc. — indicated without exception that they followed the lead of the El Capitan. But if a law were passed, it would allow them to open their doors to everyone.

One of the Smith brothers flatly said he didn't allow "colored" people in his establishment because it would be bad for his business. He claimed that ten years ago, he lost some white customers "who complained that we were serving Indians and niggers, and said would take their business elsewhere."

"How many white persons complained?" I asked.

"I don't remember how many," he answered, "but it was more than two or three."

I asked him if he would follow a law if it was passed, and he begrudgingly agreed: "If it were passed." That answer was all that I wanted for the record.

The base commander didn't use his economic clout to oppose segregation either. Instead, he bragged that two civilian minorities — one American Indian and one black — served in supervisory capacities. The district attorney offered an already familiar explanation about no qualified Negroes applying for any county positions. A county commissioner argued "the only thing that is going to cure this problem is time. No law is going to force good will."

One significant item was brought to light by the high school principal: The school system wasn't segregated. All of the children went to school together, but after school they could not enjoy the social amenities together. 'What a demeaning thing to do to a person,' I thought. I would later find this to be the case in other areas of the state.

After ten hours of this testimony broken up only by a box lunch, I was ready to leave the "friendly" city of Hawthorne, Nevada.

The next day, United Press International led its coverage of the meeting with this: " 'The only way to eliminate racial discrimination in Nevada is to pass more effective laws in the legislature,' Bob Bailey, chairman of the Nevada Commission on Equal Rights, said yesterday . . .

"Bailey accused county officials of a 'complete lack of interest' in supporting the state's public policy of nondiscrimination. 'The majority of businessmen would welcome corrective legislation which would put them all on an equal basis,' he said. 'This legislation is needed so Hawthorne will not continue to be called 'the Mississippi of the West.'"

I was relieved to know the next hearing was in Las Vegas, where we would be in a different atmosphere. Our 1960 initiative had done worlds of good, but there was still work to be done in the areas of employment, housing, banking, and public accommodations on Fremont Street, where some of the casinos were still using the old "we reserve the right to refuse service" dodge to continue discrimination.

We scheduled two days of hearings, and I was a little nervous about what kind of response we would get to our invitations. I did not want to subpoena the movers and shakers unless we had to. Fortunately, responses came quickly, with the sheriff and the district attorney the first to accept. That was a big relief, since away from this committee I was still a radio and TV guy who did business with some of the people I would be questioning.

I treated everyone with respect, but stayed firm in getting to the issues. The next two days brought out testimony from every facet of state government: law enforcement, the fire department, the school district, and Nellis Air Force Base. But the main focus was on the hotel and casino industry, because that's where most of the jobs were. The trade unions representing a vast majority of that work force gave testimony that sometimes conflicted with the hotel executives about whether any blacks were on their rosters.

Of particular significance was the testimony given by Primas White, who was the first president of the laborer's union. His work provided great opportunities for the inclusion of minority laborers in the construction fields.

Our commission had asked the Gaming Control Board to require its license holders to abide by the public policy or face a fine, perhaps even revocation. They responded in no uncertain terms that they would not do any such thing; that it was beyond their mandate to police anything other than the regulations covering gaming. This answer prompted me to demand the licensees appear before us and testify about how closely they were following the agreement which cancelled the march in 1960. Instead, they sent their attorneys and promised to make the next session, before the legislative meeting.

The banking community had a very sorry record of economic support on their lending and employment practices. They offered up the same old story: No qualified blacks ever applied for jobs, and few, if any, applied for loans. I knew this wasn't true; I helped a few people put loan applications together, only to see them turned down for frivolous reasons. One excuse was the lack of a credit record, which you could not establish without first being given credit — a vicious circle!

I had to hide my anger and, as the kids would say, "keep my cool." I had to remember this wasn't a courtroom. What the hearings did was put the system on notice that all testimony was on the record, and at some point in the future it could be challenged. Every claim of an open-door policy could become the target of a test case. When it was all said and done, I had probably signed more subpoenas than the Kefauver Commission that investigated organized crime in the casino industry. We were able to open a public dialogue and make a lot of people look ridiculous when they said there were no black candidates qualified to be waiters, desk clerks, or bellmen. After all, blacks had been waiting on white people and carrying their baggage for one hundred years.

Some of our progress came outside the hearing room. At the Sands, Jack Entratter knew that Sammy Davis Jr. had a relationship with the Westside community. Sammy took me in to see Entratter, which helped develop a relationship between the commission and the Sands. But at other places, like the Golden Gate downtown, we had to fight tooth and nail.

We finally saw the passage of the state equal rights law, the Nevada version of the landmark Civil Rights Law of 1964, which was passed just prior to the legislative session where we asked for ours. Lawmakers knew they might as well pass one and make Nevada a "deferral state" that would satisfy federal law; otherwise the feds would be in the state looking into their business. At least that was the way I sold it. I said, "Either we clean our own linen or we let Washington clean it for us. I want to take care of my state, but if you don't, then I gotta scream to the man in Washington."

That was followed by a consent decree in November 1969. The Justice Department came into the area and, from all the evidence of overt discrimination, determined they were going to take all the Las Vegas casinos and unions to court on discrimination charges. That brought about an agreement to put an affirmative action program together, with goals of twelve percent employment in various categories and three years to implement it. It was a binding agreement, and that's really how blacks got in to work, even though our efforts had opened a few doors in the '60s. The truth is that it has consistently been the law that brought about desegregation.

A few years later, I was appointed director of the Manpower Program, a new employment program for the poor and minorities. We went to work taking inventory of jobs in town that were not available to our black and brown clients, and I wrote a program for the U.S. Labor Department, proposing the department pay wages for thirteen weeks if the employer would consider hiring our candidate after the training period. We were doing okay with one-on-one placement, but I wanted something more widespread.

One night, I watched an interview with Jay Sarno, the impresario who built Las Vegas' first two fantasy-themed properties, Caesars Palace and Circus-Circus. He mentioned how hard it was to keep good workers on the second-level carnival midway at Circus. Bingo! Did I have an idea for Jay.

A couple of days later, I was giving him my proposal. Summer was both a vacation break for local students and a time of busy family traffic for Circus-Circus. What about an "on the job" training program with a fifty percent salary share through the federal programs? The midway was perfect for the young trainees, because it wasn't part of the casino or alcohol-serving operation. The Labor Department had never funded a program of this type before, but they liked the part of my sales pitch that pointed out the program would take black and Hispanic teens off the street during the hot summer months.

Sarno agreed, and we put sixty young people to work. At the end of the summer, some of them went back to school and others were retained. The program was eventually taken over by the Employment Security Agency.

Later, I also started a minority casino dealers school and telecommunications school. Couple these efforts with the work that was being done by the Equal Rights Commission and NAACP, and you could see the forces of fair play were finally surfacing in our state.

Chapter 7

Opportunities Lost

It's amazing how the birth of children can change the way you see things, make you reassess your purpose and plans for the future. Johnny was born in April of 1960, just one month after the threatened march on the Strip, and our daughter Kimberly was born in May of 1962, the year the commission hearings took place. I guess it wasn't surprising, given my work on the commission, that Anna wanted both babies to be delivered in a San Francisco hospital she had scouted during her show travels.

To say their births at this juncture in my life was symbolic is like saying the sun will rise every day. Both my heart and my mind were opening up to the possibilities of change in their world, even though those possibilities seemed to be hanging from the thin threads of promises made by men and women with all the control. After listening to hours of testimony about the blatant segregation in our hotels, unions, banks, governments, and schools, I would come home and look at these beautiful babies and think, 'God willing, it will be a different world for you.' They deserved a future, I would say to myself, as bright and full of promise as any other child.

Even as the work on the commission continued, my growing family also made me realize I had some very practical concerns. I needed to support them, and while my TV and radio work was going strong, it wasn't enough. I decided to take a real estate course at the University of Nevada, Las Vegas, and eventually obtained a broker's license. I was the first African American to hold one in Las Vegas, and probably the state, but it wasn't long before my friends Margie Elliot and Lloyd Bryant, a savvy businessman who had a dry cleaning business and several other ventures in the black community, also obtained their licenses.

My real estate business took hold, and I will always be grateful for the housing legislation passed by Congress and reinforced by the courts at that time. For decades, private-property owners from Seattle to Chicago had been using deed restrictions to spell out who could and couldn't purchase homes in their neighborhoods based on race, ethnicity, or religion. Las Vegas was certainly part of that. There was no such thing as moving into a white neighborhood if you were African American. During the equal rights' hearings, we listened to several complaints about the barriers put up against minorities looking for homes beyond the Westside, and learned that the local board of realtors was turning a blind eye to these grievances. The Fair Housing Act of 1968 and a U.S. Supreme

Court decision that same year helped clarify housing biases and gave the laws some teeth. Finally, the Federal Housing Administration (FHA) was helping to ensure that minorities and the poor were receiving home loans.

My steps into the business world took off into other directions as well during the 1960s. In some cases, it was a matter of necessity, at other times the ventures reflected a long-held belief that it was vital to give back — that old sense of responsibility tapping me on the shoulder again. The most successful long-term project was Sugar Hill, a nightclub and liquor store developed and operated with members of my extended family — the Baileys, the McClendons (my sister and her husband), Mrs. Porters (Anna's mother), and the Regans (Anna's sister and her family) — who were starting to migrate to Las Vegas. I wanted to give them something that would provide a steady living, something we could build up together. My sister, for instance, had been an assistant manager at a major department store in Ohio, but I knew she would never be able to find something similar in Las Vegas because of job discrimination.

The name was chosen to convey a feeling of sophistication. Sugar Hill is an upscale neighborhood in New York City's Harlem, and also the name of the musical I was in years earlier in Los Angeles. Our version of Sugar Hill opened at Carey and Lexington, in a newer area of town called Vegas Heights. It was originally a neighborhood for whites, so I was among the first African Americans to open a business in the area.

We built the nightclub from the ground up, then acquired the house next door and turned it into a liquor store with pool tables. We even had an outdoor garden area where we showed movies. We opened in 1965. Anna managed the place, did all the banking, and ordering. She'd work behind the counter if a clerk didn't show up, or grab a mop if the janitor wasn't around.

Entertainers from the Strip would come over to the nightclub after their performances and jam until 6 or 7 AM, just like the old days on Jackson Avenue. Johnny Carson would show up and play the drums all night. Depending on the night, he could have been cheered on by Sammy Davis Jr., Duke Ellington, Fats Domino, or Sonny Liston. People living on the other side of town didn't think twice about hopping into a cab and coming to the club.

In the meantime, I was also looking for ways to bring some development to the Westside by using the contacts I had made through my real estate business, TV show, and community work. I knew the city was growing and there was potential.

One of my first ideas was the creation of a tourist attraction called The Three Continents. It would focus on the food, clothing, and artifacts of Africa, Asia, and South America, much like Mexican villages and Chinatown concepts in other cities. This one, however, would bring three continents together in one place. I worked presentations for banks and community organizations. Everyone seemed to like the idea, but no one wanted to invest. I even went to Washington DC, to talk with representatives from the Small Business Administration at the Department of Commerce about its new Equal Opportunity Loan

Program. The conversations were stimulating, but there was no money for a project such as mine.

One of the problems was that I wanted to bring in slot machines as a major source of income for the attraction, but the SBA could not legally take part in a loan that was tied to gaming. The banks, on the other hand, thought it too much of a risk to approve the loan without the guarantee of revenue from slots. I was in a Catch-22. The project never got off the ground.

But there are always opportunities out there. You just have to know when to grab onto them. One afternoon, I received a flier from the FHA about a government-backed loan program for building housing in low-income areas. I was constantly looking for programs that would apply to the Westside and knew there was a short supply of quality housing. I immediately called the local FHA director and set up a meeting. Based on the meeting, I knew this was doable and believed it would fill a niche in the community. The development of single-family housing had been on the rise, but multi-family apartments had not. The government had built some public housing units, but here was this market in the middle, between public housing and home ownership, that was not being served. That was where our project would fit in.

The first step was to put together a corporation with eight individuals and myself. We came up with a name, Forward Look Apartments, to convey the concept of safe, decent, and affordable housing for the Westside.

It was a rocky beginning. Most of us had never worked on the governing board of a business; the closest any of us had come was volunteering on nonprofit church councils.

But we managed to finish the project, building a beautiful two-story complex with one, two, and three-bedroom apartments and a swimming pool on a plot of land off North H Street.

The first year went smoothly. I managed the project out of my real-estate office and received two percent of the rental receipts. This percentage was set by the FHA and did not begin to cover the time required for the job or office expenses. But the program did demand a certain amount of self-reliance in the pursuit of building up your own neighborhood. In the meantime, dissension and misunderstandings plagued our corporate meetings and my management fee became a major issue of contention. Tired of arguments about finance and administration, along with having to do the maintenance, I finally offered to turn the administrative duties over to two of the main protagonists in this drama, a mistake I would regret the rest of my professional life. I allowed my ego to take over, resenting the lack of gratitude for putting this whole project together. And through my frustration, I let go of the management job instead of fighting to keep it. But even as I walked away, a gnawing voice inside was saying, 'These two have no experience in housing management. They are going to be in trouble.' And I was right.

Within six months, the mortgage wasn't getting paid. By the end of a year, we were in foreclosure. The FHA took ownership of the building and eventually tore it down. It was the only major housing project members of the black community had created at that time on the Westside, and it had been destroyed by in-fighting.

The apartments were eventually replaced by the True Love Missionary Baptist Church, which still stands there today. I can remember driving past the church not long after it was built, thinking, 'All they want us to do is pray.' I knew it was also God's hope that we would make things better by helping ourselves.

Another apartment complex built in the area around that time still stands today. It was owned by a white real estate group and, while it also suffered some setbacks, the FHA gave them a grace period so they could refinance and capture some of the families that had to move from the Forward Look Apartments. A coincidence? Maybe.

I RECEIVED AN UNEXPECTED CALL FROM A prominent lawyer in town a mover-and-shaker who represented the power structure in the area. He gave out no clues over the phone, so I spent the next few days chasing ideas around in my head like a kid trying to guess what he was going to find under the Christmas tree. 'Maybe he wants my advice on some new housing development,' I thought, 'or my counsel on a new black-oriented hotel. A new hotel and casino. A new Moulin Rouge. That's it!'

The day finally arrived and I headed to the lawyer's office dressed in my Western garb, knowing he'd be wearing his, and took a seat in the lobby next to a man who introduced himself as Bob Keltonbourne. I knew Bob by reputation as was one of the largest landowners in the valley. This was high cotton. He said he recognized me from my work on the Equal Rights Commission and TV.

As the conversation continued, it became clear we were both there for the same meeting. When we were finally led into the lawyer's office all I could think was, 'This is big.'

We wasted no time getting down to business. After a few pleasantries, the lawyer turned to me.

"Bob, there's a new program the government's come up with. Any commercial real estate or business located in an area that experienced the effects of the riot could sell that property to a minority, and receive a tremendous tax break."

Before he could continue, Keltonbourne looked me straight in the eye and said, "How would you like to own the West Owens Shopping Center?"

I was shocked. It took me a few seconds to absorb what they were saying.

"What is this going to cost me?" I shot back.

I knew about the tax-break program but this was a major piece of property. In fact, it was the largest piece of commercial property in the Westside.

"We'll make it work for you," the lawyer said.

He then winked at me, and Keltonbourne smiled. The deal was on.

Keltonbourne held the second mortgage on the property and First Western held the first. I asked for all the financial information, including debt service and operating expenses. I also asked them to give me a few days to put pencil to paper and see if I could make it work.

The riot they were talking about was sparked by the famous black uprising in the Los Angeles neighborhood of Watts. On August 11, 1965, long-simmering resentment between residents and the local police finally came to a head. The explosion spilled over to Las Vegas. Rioters targeted stores on the Westside, breaking windows, stealing, and setting a few fires, which were quickly contained. Some of them ran through the shopping center, stealing from tenants such as Western Auto and damaging signs along the front of the buildings. Repairs still needed to be made and there were also quite a few empty rental spaces due, in part, to a lack of investor confidence after the incident.

The center was divided into three buildings. The largest tenant, a community services program called the Economic Opportunity Board, had its own 20,000-square-foot complex. There also was an Elks Lodge, and several retail businesses ranging from a meat market to a drug store. Of the 100,000 square feet of space, sixty percent of it was rented. It all penciled out at break-even if all the tenants made their payments on time. If we could rent the additional 20,000 square feet and get the refurbishing behind us, the property could make a nice profit. I went to the bank with my financial proposal, which included a second round of financing after eighteen months, and it was accepted.

The first year went smoothly. But then I got notice from the EOB that they were moving out; the state had a building that was available for half the rent. Suddenly, I had to figure out what I was going to do with 20,000 square feet of space. Replacing the EOB wasn't going to be easy; some businesses were moving out of the neighborhood due to fear of another racially-charged uprising.

At that time, in the mid 1960s, discrimination still lingered in the Las Vegas community. Despite the recent legislation to confront the issue, we still had a long way to go. Around the same time I was looking for a new tenant, the local NAACP was trying to find a hotel to host its annual fundraiser. While some of the hotels didn't refuse their reservation outright, they did say the meeting rooms were booked on the requested dates. I agreed to talk to some of the hotel executives I had met through my TV work or the state commission. The first hotel still turned us down, but the second — a hotel on Fremont Street — agreed to give us the space.

It embarrassed me to have to intercede when the hotels should have given the same respect to our chairperson. I remember thinking, 'You always need to have your own places that *you* control.' And that's when it hit. I had 20,000 square feet of space just waiting to be used. I would build my own meeting place: an auditorium and casino.

That moment of clarity was a huge rush. My whole body shivered. The more I thought about it, the more exciting it became. The market was there. More African Americans were coming to town. Jackson Avenue was still alive and together. But this venue would go way beyond anything being offered on Jackson. This would be a venture to bring a wide scope of jobs to the community, attract new businesses and, as a byproduct, solve the problem of trying to find that elusive tenant. The final piece of the puzzle was my late-night television show, *The Rounders' Club*, which would be a great vehicle for publicizing the new auditorium, just as it had been instrumental for Sugar Hill.

I moved forward fairly quickly, contacting some friends who came in as partners, including Buck West and James McMillan, applying for a nonrestrictive gaming license, and hiring an architect and structural engineers to handle the building's renovation. The day after the EOB moved out, we began construction.

The project had many facets. It would serve as both a meeting place for the local community and a chance for a black investment group to establish itself as an equal player in the gaming industry. Finally, it would be ours: a major project owned and operated by the Las Vegas African American community.

In coming up with a name for the center, we looked for something that would fit the community profile and make a statement at the same time. This was a business venture, first and foremost, but there was also a need in the area for a sense of heritage. We wanted to feed the soul, you might say. We discussed how different African nations during that period were getting their independence, and touched upon the fact that discrimination was being confronted in cities across the country. The name, for us, was a natural: The Pan-Afro Auditorium.

When the building was complete, we even hung colorful African flags around the perimeter and printed brochures with information about each country. When children came by, we would hand them the pamphlets and tell them to come back in a week. For every flag they could identify by country and leader, they would get a dollar.

During construction, some of the employees from Channel 8, friends of mine who believed in the project, came by to help set up the lighting and sound systems. The auditorium was large enough to seat about 5,000 but we also had separation walls so it could be broken up into three different sections. The casino area included a poker room enclosed in glass so that everyone was part of the excitement, two blackjack tables, twenty-one slot machines, a craps table, and a cocktail lounge called the Mau Mau Room.

But as opening day neared, I grew more and more anxious. The partners I was depending on to run the casino, all of them dealers from other properties, were slowing everything down; failing to submit the necessary paperwork for obtaining a gaming license and basically putting a halt to the project. I tried to meet with all nine of them one day. Only two showed up. I was crushed. Was it jealousy? One of them could have been part of a plan to undermine the project, which would escalate his ability to take over if I failed. There never was a clear explanation as to why they backed out at the last minute, but it was highly suspect. This was supposed to be a vehicle owned and operated by African Americans, the same way Jews, Italians, the Chinese, and other cultures put their talent and money together to instill pride among their own. It was a chance to compete in the system, to stand on our own two feet and say, "We can do it, too."

There was no way to turn back the clock. I had to keep moving, even though I knew nothing about operating a gaming business. Just forty-five days prior to the opening, I still needed to hire the shift managers and dealers for the poker room. In the end, I had to put my trust in the general manager of the casino.

In the meantime, I knew about entertainment and promotion. I started planning musical events for the local churches and concerts every month, bringing in entertainers such as Ray Charles, blues singer Bobby "Blue"

Bland, jazz organist Jimmy Smith, and James Cleveland, a gospel singer, arranger and composer. I also organized a handful of other events, including a gala to salute the local pastors in town, and a telethon to raise money for sickle cell anemia research. But as the months passed, it was getting harder to come out ahead. The Pan-Afro was barely holding its own. The shopping center's roofs and air conditioners were in dire need of repair. Insurance rates had doubled because of the riots and some of the tenants were hedging on their rent. It was time to rework my projections and go back for the second round of financing.

I went back to First Western Savings and Loan with my new estimates, but didn't hear from anyone for about two weeks. I finally called. It turned out the bankers I had worked with before, including the president, were no longer employed there. A sick feeling came to the pit of my stomach. When I did finally get an appointment, it was a disaster. The new president, General Taylor, didn't think the Pan-Afro was a good risk and found every reason not to honor the commitment his predecessor had made to me. I tried other banks and got a similar reaction. Even Bob Keltonbourne was less than enthusiastic when I approached him as a final act of desperation. As I drove by the center one day, and looked at those beautiful flags flying atop the Pan-Afro Auditorium, I said to myself, 'If it's for me, it will work out. If not, I'll write it off and move on.'

The holidays were approaching and like a lot of businesses, particularly those in the service industry, we were looking forward to a lucrative New Year's Eve. I decided I could buy some time with the receipts and approach some other investors to keep the place above water. I talked to two business owners on Jackson Avenue, but they didn't have the cash to jump into another venture. Then I approached two operators from the downtown area, one of whom was Jack Binion, son of the local legend Benny Binion. I must say, Jack did come over to check out the Pan-Afro, and he complimented me on its layout. But he had no interest in taking part. He was nervous, he said, about doing business in the black area of town because the El Morocco, a Jackson Avenue club owned by a white partner of his, had to close because of a bad experience. I never cease to become annoyed when people take one failure and use that experience as a reason to turn down another project in a minority neighborhood.

New Year's Eve came and we did quite well, hosting revelers until the sun came up. The cash receipts were counted and locked up in the safe. I headed for home, promising my manager I would return in a few hours to relieve him from his duties.

The success of the evening had given me a lift, particularly after weeks of trying to find ways to save the business. I stopped by Sugar Hill on the way home to see how it had fared that night and the news was good. When I got to the house I gave Anna a hug, kissed my children, then went straight to bed. A few hours later I was roused by a phone call from a Pan-Afro employee requesting that I head down to the casino to give some chips to the poker room and lock up the cash. I asked where the manager was, because I knew he had a small safe he could use to keep the cash out of sight until I could take care of it later.

"He went to get something to eat and said he would be back in an hour, and that was five hours ago," the employee said. "In fact, he left right after you did."

I went to the club, headed straight for the office and spotted the small safe with its door wide open. All the contents inside were gone. The blood drained from my face. I immediately went to the larger safe and it was the same story. All the paper currency and some of the chips I had placed inside had been taken. Now I was numb. The manager had robbed me blind. Suddenly, I began to remember the small suspicions I used to have, that he had been looking over my shoulder when I dialed the combination on the safe. I called the police and they took fingerprints off both safes but that was about all they could do.

The next few days were a nightmare. My chips were on the street, $2,500 worth, and the company was responsible for the cash value to be paid upon demand of the customer. I closed down the live-gaming operation and put the poker tables on a cash basis with no new release of chips. The ones in the streets would be the only chips left in circulation. The manager probably sold them to some of the players for a portion of their face value, and it would take about a month for them to show up. Indeed, a couple of people actually came in and tried to cash the stolen chips, holding maybe $500 each. I didn't pay them. They said they could file complaints with the Nevada Gaming Commission. "Go ahead," I said. They were never heard from again.

I used Sugar Hill money to keep afloat. The overhead and the loss of more than $35,000 in cash had tapped me out. I also put more effort into trying to get investors involved in a business that still could become a cash cow even though I was over a barrel at the time. A few offers came in to buy Sugar Hill, but I turned them down. It was a business that involved extended family, and the sustenance for some very loyal employees. Eventually came the cold realization that the times just weren't open to a dream like mine: a project for my own people. Some also may have seen it as a threat, including the casinos on Fremont, which had finally opened their doors to blacks and, ironically, may have been afraid of losing their new customers.

In the end, the Pan-Afro closed after nine months. Eventually, I found out why First Western had refused to honor their financial commitment. Another group of young black brothers was waiting in the background to take over the center once my foreclosure period expired. They would not honor the lease I had put together between me, as owner of the Pan-Afro Auditorium, and the shopping center corporation, which was a separate entity. They threatened to sue if I tried to hold the new owners to the lease. Their deep pockets would certainly outlast my resources. I had lost enough money fighting for what was born as an important community resource.

On my last night as owner of the Pan-Afro, I switched on the building's outside lights, then sat in my car looking at the auditorium. I pulled out a flask of cognac and took a drink, leaned back, and lit a cigarette. Thoughts of the past several weeks came flooding in.

The manager was never caught, so I didn't have the luxury of seeing him behind bars. A few years later, we heard he was in some kind of trouble in Los Angeles, but that's all I ever found out. The police told me he was a pro. Pro or not, I carried a .38-caliber pistol on my side for about a month, hoping I would run into him. I suppose it's a good thing I didn't. As it was, his disappearance made him as tangible as smoke, nothing but the terrible memory of an open door to an empty safe. The anger would linger for a very long time.

But I also thought about the relationships I made through the venture and the excitement of starting the project. There was always something else out there, some other way to make a difference. Recently, I had been asked to direct a government-subsidized job program for minorities and the poor in the city. And there was an issue very close to my heart: developing the Westside. If we could only break down the resistance of the banks toward providing capital to minority-owned businesses and start-ups . . . I put the flask away and started up the car. It was time to get back to work.

Chapter 8

Minority Business in America, Nevada Style

THE CRY OF BLACK CAPITALISM WAS ALIVE IN Washington DC President Nixon had endorsed a program to assist minority entrepreneurial start-ups and the strengthening of management capabilities by establishing a new agency called the Office of Minority Business Enterprise, housed in the Department of Commerce. In his special message to Congress in March 1972, Nixon wrote, "Potential minority entrepreneurs are eager to join the mainstream of the nation's commerce. . . . The principal need of minority business today is for a greater supply of investment capital."

My recent experiences were a stinging reminder of just how true this was. Civil rights had made great strides on the social front, but the movement hadn't reached the capital community. And that's what cuts you off at the knees. If you can't have access to capital in a capitalistic society, you're dead. When I went in to the shopping center project, I knew I would need second-tier financing. I wouldn't have taken the loan in the first place if I hadn't been assured (alas, with a "handshake" deal, but not on paper) that secondary financing would follow at a given point.

All this was still fresh in my mind the day I got a message to call back Alan Bible, our veteran U.S. Senator from Nevada. 'What's this about?' I wondered. It wasn't election season and no one was threatening to riot on the Westside. Must be important.

It was. "Bob, I have something I think would be right up your alley," he said. The veteran senator had remembered my efforts to develop the Three Continents attraction in the black area. "I've got the answer to your concerns about the terrible conditions the minority entrepreneur faces in this country."

He began to explain the OMBE program as a mechanism to address these issues. "I'd like you to become acquainted with this program, representing Nevada on my behalf. I'm sending your name over to the Department of Commerce and you can expect a call."

Within a week, the director was inviting me to come to Washington to attend a training session at Howard University. The session was for future directors who would start and manage companies within a national network of Business Development Centers. There would be one hundred of these centers around the country, and Las Vegas stood a good chance to get one of them. This center would provide assistance to minorities in all phases, from start-ups to expansion, and identify procurement opportunities in all projects that received federal funding. There was also training for money management, loan packaging, and bidding for contract opportunities. Bible, being the chairman of the Senate Small Business Committee, would have a lot of clout in the oversight of this effort.

The training course at Howard University was a lot of work, but the thrill of starting the uphill battle of fiscal empowerment was inspiring. My real estate and business experience would be called upon to create a center in Las Vegas. After returning home, the next few days found me developing information to be used in the proposal for our center. I was under the impression that I would get the contract on a "sole source" basis, and not have to go through a bidding process. Wrong. The Department of Commerce had to advertise and put it out for bid. But when I read the bid specifications, I relaxed. The training from the six-week session at Howard had paved a path of preparation.

Getting the blessing of the minority community was another matter. The NAACP was still the major group representing African Americans, and El Circulo Cubano spoke for most of the Hispanics. Trying to head off a tug of war, I called representatives from both organizations to meet and hear my proposal. Both groups knew me from the Equal Rights Commission, so it wasn't like a stranger was approaching them. I outlined a plan to balance the power: Neither group would hold the two positions of director and deputy director at the same time. The board of directors also would include representation of the county's various minority groups. Everyone was on the same page. NEDCO, the Nevada Economic Development Company, was born.

We incorporated as a non-profit agency and prepared a proposal that trumped those from other organizations. NEDCO became the first minority business development center in Nevada. Our mission was to assist minority owned companies (those with fifty-one percent ownership or more) and teach them to be competitive. I chose office space on Sixth Street in downtown Las Vegas, within walking distance of the major banks. I wanted it to be known that NEDCO wasn't a welfare service, but a capital development company, so we should be near the capital resources.

We started workshops on construction management and the bidding process, drawing upon what I learned at Howard. Most of the initial training was how to properly structure a loan package and a business plan. In most cases, our clients had the product skills but not the management experience. With our limited resources, we decided to focus seventy percent of the effort on existing businesses in retail and construction and the rest on new starts. In essence, the program included not just federal agencies and government contractors, but any organization that was using government funds. In fact, most of the initial resistance was from the agencies themselves.

They hadn't been brought up to speed on the changes as quickly as I had been in my Washington crash course.

The new federal guidelines helped us with early success stories such as John Wesley, who came through our door as a one-man trucking company. He would haul materials to construction sites and pick up their trash. But he didn't have "relationships" with the unions, and they didn't want to let him into a very close-knit family of haulers. John was the kind of guy you didn't mind going to bat for, because he could deliver the goods and didn't take no for an answer. But it wasn't easy for him to get exposure at the time, and the prime contractors found all kind of reasons not to accept his bids.

Our secret weapon turned out to be a federal stipulation that a bid from a minority contractor would have an automatic ten percent reduction. This "set-aside" made John's bids harder to ignore, and we appealed to the Department of Transportation to provide ongoing support for him and make sure the major contractors gave him an opportunity to compete. We helped John market his company and establish lines of credit. Today the Wesley Corporation is one of the biggest trucking operators in Nevada, with forty to seventy employees.

NEDCO quickly took root as a support mechanism for minority entrepreneurs. Much of our program centered in on working capital and bonding, two of the requirements for doing business with the public sector and also something aspiring subcontractors need to get jobs from the major contractors. Bonding companies don't like companies with little experience, or marginal lines of credit. Congress moved to pass legislation to establish bonding assistance, supporting the subcontractor entrepreneurs for one year. This effort was close to my heart, as I believe that making opportunity available to everyone brings about a more competitive marketplace, and then everyone benefits.

THE NEXT ELEMENT WAS ACCESS TO INFORMAtion. OMBE held regional and national meetings for its business development centers. Even so, one of the major concerns was the lack of information the federal agencies and prime contractors were sharing with the OMBE programs. This was a serious problem that deserved some serious attention. My marketing sensibilities began to boil. We had access to a good conference, but the information we gleaned from the agencies would be second or third hand by the time we passed it on to our clients. Why not give a conference for the entrepreneurs themselves? Bring the job opportunities to them first hand? The NEDCO Procurement Conference was born.

We proposed the conference as an outreach vehicle for the minority business community, using funding the OMBE had offered for any new ideas that enhanced the delivery system. We brought the federal agencies and the prime contractors to Las Vegas to spend two to three days identifying potential procurement opportunities with them. The conference was a win/win for everyone concerned. It not only provided information for the minority entrepreneurs, but it also gave the agencies and prime contractors a chance to comply with the minority outreach goals they were supposed to accomplish. The regional director bought the idea, funded it, and we were off and running.

In 1976, we approached Caesars Palace with a proposal for a regional conference that would draw between one hundred-fifty and two hundred people. Caesars was the hottest hotel going at the time and would be a draw in itself, on top of the program content. Hotel management seemed a bit hesitant at first, but they finally agreed to a date in December, which was the slowest time of the year for tourism. Some of our government sponsors originally felt that the gambling and glamour of Las Vegas would detract from the serious business of the meetings. Wrong. Workshops were at maximum attendance. And the hospitality suite Caesars gave us added an extra luster of "big-time" treatment to the affair, especially when the costumed Caesar and Cleopatra greeters posed for photos with conferees in their full Roman attire.

I knew this conference would grow and establish NEDCO as a major player in the country's minority business growth — and it did. Each year was an improvement over the previous one, and we were able to involve some of the clients we helped get started. Willard Booth was the owner of Lucky Seven Limo Service, and gave our conference speakers and VIPs a taste of true Vegas hospitality, and the class we pursued at each of our gatherings.

Occasionally, I would take some of the players out to Sugar Hill to get a flavor of Las Vegas life away from the Strip. I didn't make a big play for the action, because I didn't want to be accused of using the conference for my own personal benefit. My inside buddies from California and Washington were familiar with "the Hill" and found their way out there to hear the jazz and blues, and sample the best steak burger and barbequed rotisserie chicken in town. When I missed the regulars at the hospitality suite, I knew where they were. It wasn't that Caesars didn't offer great entertainment. It's just that you sometimes get a cultural calling and have to hear some funky blues and jazz.

The first four regional conferences were such a success that the various agencies encouraged me to look into having it go national. The expansion would require more funding for marketing and staff. I got the support of the national office and the Small Business Administration. Everyone was quite excited about the potential of a national conference.

All we needed now was a host property. I had moved the fourth of our regional conferences to the Desert Inn, which boasted its own golf course, but also had a conservative reputation. I met with Burton Cohen, the chief operating officer, and shared my vision, laying out what facilities and special room rates I would need for five hundred to seven hundred people. Cohen agreed to it all, and instructed his publicity director to give us any help we needed. It helped that Cohen was a jazz buff, so there was some basis of common ground and it wasn't just strictly business.

It took a lot of work to get this thing off the ground, and some of the staff and coordinators who helped went all the way back to the Moulin Rouge days: Alice Key and Martha Jordan (Louis' wife and a dancer with Anna in the circuit days) among them. This greeting I wrote for the conference's second year summed up the spirit of that first gathering: "Repeat after me: 'I am a Capitalist! I am in business to make a profit! I don't want a handout — just an opportunity!'"

The conference emphasized equal opportunity through equal access to information. It was a "buy-sell" arena designed to bring entrepreneurs face to face with the movers and shakers of both the federal and private sectors. It wasn't designed for "undisciplined dreamers or unrealistic entrepreneurs," I wrote, but for those willing to sharpen their edge in the competitive world. President Reagan greeted the conference with a videotaped welcome. Though I had worked hard to get White House support, I had no idea my request, through Senator Paul Laxalt, would produce a message delivered by the President himself.

Of course, our meeting dovetailed perfectly with Reagan's commitment to minority business. In the summer before we convened, July 1983, he signed an executive order requiring all federal departments and agencies to develop annual minority business enterprise plans. NEDCO had produced a product addressing the expectations of all participants. More than a billion dollars in procurement opportunities had been identified. It was a slam-dunk, and everyone agreed, "same time next year." Our national conferences went on five more years, through 1988.

THE MOST ACCEPTABLE METHODS OF GETTING contracts was through the Small Business Administration's

8(a) program, which was formed to help small companies owned and operated by "socially and economically disadvantaged persons," in the words of the statute. The other route was through subcontracts with the prime contractors who were subject to "set-aside" program guidelines.

We started a concentrated probe on the largest single budget in the government, the Department of Defense; specifically, the MX Missile program. We got a lot of help from Congressman Parren Mitchell, the first African American elected from Maryland. His leadership provided hope when the MBE programs seemed to falter. He spoke periodically at the conferences, and when he wasn't there he sent special counsel Major Clark to give a heads up on new legislation that would affect our programs negatively.

The Department of Transportation was the next big challenge. The state DOT operated without involving any minority or female-owned companies. This was going to be a hard nut to crack, but we were ready for it. We formed another company, a sister company to NEDCO called New Ventures, just to cover Department of Transportation activities in the state. We put it under the direction of Horacio Lopez, deputy director of NEDCO. I wrote the proposal with the aid of NEDCO data. This effort was funded by the U.S. Department of Transportation. We kept both operations under the same roof so the clients could come to our "one-stop shopping center."

Lopez took the reigns and put the program in gear. He had learned a lot about the construction industry and the state's bidding process through NEDCO. The state Department of Transportation was accepting its federal obligations, but the big problem for minorities was the expensive investment for equipment required to perform the major construction work. So we opted to identify the sub-contracting possibilities most feasible to go after. We made suggestions that opened up new areas of highway-related needs, such as flagging, road signs, and training for heavy-duty driving equipment.

One of our clients, Lou Richardson, was an accomplished engineer, and we used him to open doors with the Department of Transportation on highway work. He was really qualified, but we had a tough time getting him recognized by the state, county and city. Richardson Construction still ended up becoming a successful company, known for building schools in Clark County. Remember, everything in the growth of Las Vegas was interrelated, and it all stemmed from personal relationships. You couldn't get in if you were not part of that circle, and certainly as a minority, you were far away from any expectation of becoming part of that circle. NDOT is a very conservative bureaucracy and doesn't like to be bothered by people outside of their own close network. In some instances, families have had two and three generations on NDOT's payroll, especially up in northern Nevada.

But again, we used the ten percent set-aside for minority bids as a wedge to get some of our people in. Sometimes, we brought people from Washington to observe the inequities and enforce the ten percent set-aside law. In some cases, the threat of bringing them in was sufficient.

We were, beyond a doubt, one of the most productive business development centers in the country. My staff is what made me look good. We didn't watch the clock for eight hours and go home. Everybody worked as long as necessary to achieve our goals.

Ernest Fountain had a banking background to offer strong leadership as director in our fiscal department. He was a brilliant young man, loyal and true, with a bright future. Our loan-packaging department was one of the best in the nation. Rob Eagan was the youngest and the fastest packager on staff, but he had a problem getting to work on time. I told him, "Come in late and stay late," to accommodate our clients who had to come in after the regular business day. It worked out fine. Ben Winslow, competent and thorough, was the pencil man for the agency and managed our fiscal reporting and audit review. He made sure the figures added up. If they didn't make sense, he would have the clients go over them until they were correct.

As our client load expanded, our staff grew. It was time to look aggressively for some female professional employees. I was fortunate to get Janet Stevenson, a crackerjack accountant, for a loan officer. She was as good with people as she was with the pencil. Our procurement program was growing and the size of the procurement opportunities was getting into the millions with the DOT jobs. New Ventures needed more technical expertise than we had in the office, so I went looking for an engineer. Luck was with me. One of our board members, Arturo Combiera, recommended a female engineer, Nora Masana. Our interview was excellent. She was both an engineer and an architect. Marilyn Cherry, for NEDCO and Karen Labot for New Ventures were the support staff, the glue that kept the companies together.

We worked as a team and gained respect within the banking circles in the town. Now it was time to make sure an infrastructure would be in place to continue our work. Lopez and Combiera worked with me in developing the framework for the Latin Chamber of Commerce. The Black Chamber was on its way. I was one of the charter members and served as president for a term. I met the president of the minority contractors association in Washington and invited him to speak at our National Procurement Conference. While he was in town, I persuaded him to let NEDCO help him to start a chapter here. It became a portion of the support system to help the contractors line up bonding and working capital. Our programs were working and we were sensitizing the business community to the presence and value of a strong minority entrepreneurial force.

By this time, I served on a lot of boards, trying to stay as close to the business organizations as possible and keep our program in front of them. I was the first African American to serve on the boards of both the Downtown Kiwanis Club and the Las Vegas Chamber of Commerce. I twice served as president of the Chamber's Prospectors, a committee of thirty longtime members who serve as the Chamber's "ambassadors." Rubbing elbows with the movers and shakers in these organizations, especially the bankers, proved to be of great help to the clients.

NEDCO was a two-sided challenge. On one end, we were marketing minority-owned businesses to a system that had not been offering opportunities to them. But on the other end, we had to make sure the minority-owned companies were ready to offer quality services and products at competitive prices delivered on time. It was a difficult job keeping that balance, and we would catch hell from both sides: Minority companies complaining about unfair treatment, and the majority-owned companies saying the clients were not delivering at a competitive price, or that the work was not up to the quality requirements. In most cases, the truth was somewhere in the middle. The companies and agencies were unhappy about being under a federal mandate, and the minority companies were angry because they were not quick to cash in on the programs' promises of new, profitable opportunities. Our job at NEDCO and New Ventures was to monitor the progress of the programs and help both sides where we could.

The gaming industry, still Nevada's major economy, was another tough nut to crack. I had contacts in all the hotels dating back to the 1950s, so I figured I knew enough people to approach them and request inclusion into the programs without a federal mandate. After a few meetings with the purchasing managers, it became apparent that I was going to need more than good will to impress them to join in the minority business drive. I had an idea that would reach out into the private sector to support the marketing efforts for our clients. I called my friend Ed Ortiz, procurement manager for Reynolds Electrical. Reynolds already was involved with the federal programs through the company's contract obligations.

"Ed, do you think you could go to your purchasing managers association and get their support to start a Las Vegas chapter of the National Minority Purchasing Council?"

As I went on to explain, the council would be a private-sector organization acting on its own to provide more business opportunities without federal dictates. A local arm of the NMPC (National Minority Purchasing Council) would, of course, include the purchasing agents for the hotels and casinos. "This would give us access to the most important person in the whole world: the buyer," I reminded him. If you could impress the buyer with your performance, you would have a chance to become a permanent supplier for that hotel. (A little Christmas gift never hurt either, we later found out.)

NEDCO and the Small Business Administration had been celebrating "Minority Business Week," a national effort that included workshops and a "marketplace day" where the companies and buyers can get together and promote their products and services. The buyers explain what they're looking for and how companies might get on the bidders list or provide a "just in time" item. The marketing cycle had now been established, forging a strong three-way alliance among NEDCO, the SBA, and the purchasing council.

I knew the MBE programs would eventually run their course and fall out of favor with the business and political forces, and that the Small Business Administration would take over the spotlight. This would not mean economic discrimination had ceased to exist, but that the programs had run their political course. Knowing this was the inevitable future, it became more important that we used the next ten years — the late 1980s and early '90s — to build an infrastructure that would continue to be available for marketing and management assistance above and beyond what the SBA would continue to give. I continued to be motivated by the notion that minority-owned entrepreneurial inclusion is a sleeping giant waiting to be properly nurtured. My love for minority business is my love for America and all that she can do to stay strong and live up to its principles. The sleeping giant moves on.

Chapter 9

The Neighborhood Changes

Las Vegas was growing up as well as outward, the white community as well as the black. There were black officials in elected offices, including district court, the county commission, and my friend Alice Key's breakthrough appointment as the state's deputy labor commissioner. Segregated housing was becoming a thing of the past. If you had the money, you could buy the house. Neighbors found it new and strange, until they came to know you as a person.

The Baileys were starting to resemble one of the suburban families you saw on TV shows. We were one of the first black families to move into Bonanza Village, which was surrounded by a depressed area, but was quite the prestigious address at the time. Though it was only a few blocks from the traditional Westside, it was a subdivision of graceful ranch houses on sprawling, one-acre lots. At first, our welcome wagon was a few eggs thrown against the house. But after a few months, people got used to us and I felt comfortable sending my son to the nearby school.

NEDCO finally paid the kind of salary I could never pull together with my TV work. Visibility on television opened all kinds of doors, but in the 1960s the Manpower program was the only way I was making any real money. When NEDCO took off, I had to give up something and it turned out to be the TV show. After 1972, I would do only special programming for another five years, including an integrated Saturday dance show on Channel 13 called *Disco Express*, inspired by *Soul Train*. The hostess for the show was the talented Florette Morgan, and it was produced by my wife, Anna Bailey.

Around the time NEDCO launched, I also had the bright idea to buy a twenty-five-foot Champion motor home for a family vacation. We would hit the road for special weekends; Johnny, about twelve, was our "engineer" with the maps, while Kim was the live wire who maintained the music and the energy level. I'll never forget one trip, when the girls got a head start to spend a week with a friend in Sausalito. The plan was for Johnny and me to meet them with the motor home for the return trip along scenic highways. We were talking, playing games, and enjoying each other's company until my engineer happened to check the gas gauge. We were almost on empty.

I started looking for the nearest sign for a gas station. The gauge was nearly on empty and there was nothing ahead but highway; no exits or signs of a service area. And it was getting dark. The gas gauge hit empty. I know there is a reserve in your tank after the peg hits rock bottom, but how far would it take us? The warning beep came on. As I was about to pull over and call for AAA or the highway patrol, we spotted a sign that said there was a gas station in two miles. The buzzer was ringing louder by the minute. We finally saw the station — on the other side of the highway, with no crossover in sight. I spotted a break in the dividing barriers that was only supposed to be used by highway workers or the highway patrol, but made a tire-squealing left turn anyway. As I rolled up to the pump and put my feet on the break, the motor coughed and died. God is good!

PERHAPS IT WAS A BITTER IRONY, BUT DESEGregation killed the Westside business district. Segregated areas across the country flourished because you had to shop, socialize, and worship in your designated section of town. Hence, you had a captured market. As substandard as some conditions might be, you had few outside options. When the walls of segregation crumbled, people had choices about where to live, shop, and socialize. Some of the black businesses tried to compete with the businesses in the majority communities, but lacked the capital to upgrade their facilities. It was time for a fresh idea and a redevelopment program. Other cities had black tourist areas; why not Vegas? We were known for good jazz music; why not a street featuring good food and good music? Call it "Jazz Alley." Much of the development was already in place, which had shifted away from the main drag on Jackson Avenue to Owens Avenue.

Reuben Bullock opened the Westside Story, which was a very fashionable supper club; probably too high fashion. After passing through a few new owners and new names, it closed. Other clubs sprouted up on Owens. Charles Kellar opened a club called the Black Orchid with good music and food. Charlie was not the most gracious host and he was at odds with the police department. He closed down in the shopping center, but later opened another place across the street; it closed after a short period. After having a place on Jackson Avenue, Sarann Knight moved over to Owens as Jackson Avenue was dying, and took over Reuben's Supper Club, changing the name to the People's Choice. She put new life in the club. Through all of the transitions of the entertainment shift from Jackson to Owens, Sugar Hill survived and became a household name with the people in the community. As I recall the history of some of the activity involving the successful operations, women were central in each one. Kitty Bruner was the backbone of Andy's Liquor Store; Sarann Knight Preddy ran the People's Choice, and later the Moulin Rouge; and my Anna Bailey, who took care of the banking, shift changes, and bills for Sugar Hill, later managed and marketed the Baby Grand.

The mayor of Las Vegas, William H. Briare, was with me in New Orleans when we received the call that the council had cancelled the funds for the continuation of the Jazz Alley project. With the unsuccessful attempts of the Alley, the action shifted.

The minority business and entertainment areas declined, except for some ethnically tailored barbershops, beauty parlors, soul food restaurants, and churches, namely Baptist churches. All the surviving Jackson Avenue buildings that once housed bars or restaurants now are churches.

Sugar Hill survived and remained a household name with the community people. For a few years, the fact that it was a mile north of the main drag, Owens Avenue — which in time had supplanted Jackson Avenue — worked against it. But in the long run, it was just as well that our bar and restaurant stood apart from the fate of the black business district. The club held its own, at least until the Los Angeles gangs moved in.

In our twenty-four years of operation, Sugar Hill had always held the underworld elements in check. They respected my community work and help to ex-convicts looking for jobs. It was a "Don't bother Bob, he helps us" attitude. However, the collapse of the Westside business district, combined with the explosion of crack cocaine in the 1980s, brought people in from out of town, including serious drug dealers.

They took over the streets, and carried on business as if they had a license to hustle any place where people gathered. It was outrageous. We pleaded for more police protection, but it was limited at best. They bought off my security guards and set up a system to warn the salesman when the police were coming. I was told that they would tip the bartender to turn his back, or go to the end of the bar so they could make a sale. I had to fire most of my security guards because they were taking money from the dope peddlers instead of taking care of me. The one good one that was left said he would have to quit, because he realized that eventually, he was either going to have to shoot somebody or be shot himself.

We faced the challenge on a day-to-day basis. I tried to talk to the troublemakers as a community brother. They would let up for a while, but then a new group would come in and it would start all over again. It got so bad until they were taking over my sidewalk around the building and threatening my manager. Everyday, the clerks were calling me at NEDCO with another problem. I started to seriously worry about my family and employees. My wife was still taking the daily receipts to the bank, my sister was still working behind the bar, and we had another lady working in the package liquor store. It became an untenable situation.

One Friday morning in 1989, I was in the middle of an important meeting when my secretary barged in and said I had an emergency call from Sugar Hill. The manager was out of breath as he explained that two of the thugs had jumped over the counter and grabbed bottles of liquor. The clerk, my sister, tried to stop them but they pushed her aside. She would have had to take the shotgun from behind the counter and blow him away or let him get away, which is what she did. I had instructed all of the clerks never to put their lives on the line to protect the store.

I had to make a quick decision. The manager was waiting on the other end of the line. I gave him a short but decisive direction. "Shut the doors. Close it up before somebody gets killed."

It was a wise decision. I later found out they were planning to rob the package store that morning, and the bar at the close of the late morning shift. Back in the early days, Sugar Hill had been worth defending with firearms. When the Los Angeles riots spread to the Westside and forced us to arm ourselves to keep the looters away from the store, the newspaper had a picture of me in front of the store with a sawed-off shotgun. I also had men positioned on the rooftops of the liquor store and restaurant. But now, it was time to look for another location in a neighborhood that would be safe for my customers as well as my employees. To this day, I salute Louis Conner for his decision to stick it out and keep his operation, Seven Seas, open for the locals.

It wasn't like I had never considered having a business close to the tourist action. In the 1960s, Nat King Cole and I tried to buy a bar that was for sale next to the Sands Hotel. The sheriff, who issued county liquor licenses, told us in no uncertain terms that he had talked to some of the hotels and they discouraged him from giving us a license. The next try was with Sammy Davis Jr. We were going to buy a place up for sale on Tropicana between Paradise and Maryland Parkway. We had so much going for us at the time, and there was nothing else in town that matched our plan for an upscale club for a black-oriented clientele. We must have been out of our minds. The bar was set on fire. Word came back that the owners said they would "burn it down before they would let those niggers have it." This was never verified, but the place was never rebuilt either.

About three months after Sugar Hill closed, Anna spotted a "For Sale" sign in front of a doctor's office on Sahara Avenue, just a block or so east of the Sahara Hotel on the Strip. Times had changed, but you can't blame me if I didn't want to test how much. I had my son Johnny, who had grown up to become an attorney, handle all of the contact with the owner. I also anticipated trouble transferring our Sugar Hill liquor license, but that went amazingly well. I guess the reputation I had built serving on all those civic groups for all those years counted for something.

The remodeling did not go as well, thanks to a complicated plan to best utilize our limited space, and the need to bring everything up to code. I also couldn't pay full attention to a contractor who had plenty of personal issues, because I was trying to launch the latest evolution of NEDCO, a company called New Ventures Development. This one would use the Small Business Administration's 504 Fixed Asset Financing Program, which provides funds for land acquisition or construction, with the lender putting up half, the Certified Development Company forty percent and the applicant ten percent.

This one was a for-profit company, though we were advised to go for non-profit status when preparing our charter. I strongly objected. "We're going into the financial hemisphere, and it operates for profit. Why should we be any different?"

The decision didn't sit well with the local office of the SBA. And I got a little nervous when another 504 application from northern Nevada, submitted before ours, was authorized before us. I went to work to utilize my relationship with Senator Paul Laxalt, and he pledged to help us. We were the first minority-owned 504 authorized lenders in the country, and this was a source of great hope. It was the financial arm we needed to strengthen NEDCO's procurement programs. Although it was a real estate development and improvement vehicle, it put us into the circle to have something to offer the banking community on a partnership basis. At last, we were in a position to develop the various types of loans our clients would need to grow. With patience and ongoing improvement in our knowledge of the real world we live in, we were moving ahead.

The bar, which we christened The Baby Grand, was moving ahead as well. And so were Anna and I. Now empty nesters, we had bought the first house for sale in The Lakes, the community built around a man-made lake stocked with catfish on the far western edge of developed Las Vegas. We were the first family to move in, right next to the model homes, with a boat dock for our back porch in the middle of the desert. And nobody could worry about me moving in, because I was there first.

Chapter 10

A Call from the Top

I was so immersed in 504 financing and trying to open the Baby Grand that I hadn't returned a call from one of our U.S. Representatives, Barbara Vucanovich. She also had helped our development company get 504 authorization, and she wanted a progress report. I had fallen behind and called her office to make amends. "That's not why she's trying to reach you," her administrator said. "But you had better let me make an appointment for her to meet with you."

What had I done now? Had I been raising too much hell with federal agencies about procurement opportunities for our clients? But the meeting was about something else entirely.

"How would you like to be a presidential appointee to the Department of Commerce?"

"Barbara, would you repeat that?"

I was familiar with the agency, because I had been contracting with them for at least fifteen years: The Minority Business Development Agency under the Department of Commerce. This was the same agency that started out as the Office of Minority Business Enterprise, the one that first trained me at Howard University to open our Las Vegas center in the 1970s.

They were looking for an associate director, and my credentials were perfect. I would be the first African American presidential appointee from Nevada. But the approval process was no piece of cake.

First, my Nevada senators and representatives have to sign off on me. No problem there. In the years after Governor Sawyer left office, I had switched back to being a Republican (though, like many Nevadans, I always pride myself on voting for individuals and not a straight party ticket). My party choice and my work in minority business put me on the radar screen of President Bush (the first one; remember it was 1989) and his Secretary of Commerce, Robert Mosbacher.

But then came the clearance process and Secret Service investigation. Before I started all this, I had to decide if I really wanted to do it. NEDCO was in full swing, New Ventures was still productive, and the New Ventures Development Company was showing great promise. I still had a real estate office, though I didn't spend much time there, and I was trying to open a new bar. I was sixty-two, three years away from the traditional retirement age. This was crazy! How many things can you do at once? At first I decided to say no to Washington.

Anna turned me around. “It’s an honor to be chosen by the president,” she reminded me, “and it will inspire other young men of color.” It would have been irresponsible, I finally decided, to not share all the information I had picked up over the years. There were only so many of us in the country who had been with the minority development program since its inception. John said he would help Anna with business decisions. Eddie, our loyal bar manager from Sugar Hill, would help Anna in the new store. So would Kim, even though she had recently had her first baby — my first grandson.

My decision only got the process started. Next came several interviews in Washington, and a little something called the White House “character and work” investigation. Three months went by after the round of interviews, and I had a sick feeling in the pit of my stomach. What would I say to all the people I had already told, perhaps prematurely, that I was on my way to Washington to be a mover and shaker?

I got a call from Kenneth Bolton, the director of the agency: “When are you going to be on board?”

“I don’t know. I thought you were calling to tell me.”

He sighed. “There’s no rushing the White House. They take their time on investigations, especially on presidential appointments.”

I got the same story from Congresswoman Vucanovich: “You don’t push these guys. They believe everyone from Nevada is suspect. They’ve been watching too many gangster movies about Las Vegas. The President has been under pressure about his appointments and they’re being extra careful about new ones, even at this level.”

All kinds of people had been calling, including friends from way back, saying they had fielded questions from investigators about my past. I had nothing to hide, but it does make you feel a little suspect when you know people are nosing into your past. Did I do anything wrong? But hey — I had been investigated for a non-restrictive gaming license in Nevada, and nobody is more thorough than the Gaming Control Board!

Finally, the call came: "You've been cleared. We need you here in two weeks." No problem. I had been packed for two months.

I had been to the Department of Commerce building many times before, but it never looked as large or as majestic as it did that first Monday I reported to work. I had to sign in before I could walk down the massive hallway. The security officer saw me trying to navigate the choice between "employees" or "guests," and helpfully volunteered that I was a guest until my identification card came in.

The waiting room in the director's office even seemed larger than it used to. The director, Ken Bolton, walked out and greeted me with a warm handshake and a big smile: "You finally got here." He introduced me around, though I already knew some of the people after doing business with this agency for so many years.

I settled in for a meeting with Ken and two new faces: deputy director Joe Lira and assistant director John Winston. (My position as an associate director rounded out Bolton's administrative cabinet.) Ken explained that he was working on a new thrust for the agency. The Bush administration had a new vision for business development, especially international business. MBDA had to figure how it would fit into the Department of Commerce's larger plan. In an October 1989 awards ceremony for the agency, Bush spoke of his intent to "to restore and reinvigorate the vision behind the (original) Office of Minority Business Enterprise" and the need to "revitalize our efforts in this regard."

As a master plan was being put together, the job at hand was to get the regional offices up to snuff and ready to run in whatever the new directions the agency would be taking. The regional directors had developed their little fiefdoms. They had total authority to audit and inspect the personnel or the files of clients they were servicing. In some cases, they were using their power to intimidate instead of acting as a support resource for the centers.

I could relate. I had been the director of one of those centers, and knew about political juice to protect our turf from regional pressure. So it made sense to assign me the job of getting the field in order. If someone had to go, it wouldn't be easy. Government employees aren't easy to get rid of. It takes at least a year to discharge a career employee; the higher the grade, the more difficult it is. All of the regional directors I would deal with were at the top level of government service rankings, and even the lower-grade employees had grieving rights. Don't get me wrong; I believe in reasonable employee protections, but not to the extent that it can stop all forward motion. But like it or not, house-cleaning was my task.

John Winston put me up for a few nights while I looked for a place to live. We hit it off right away, because we had similar backgrounds in music and TV. He had been a singer, a drummer, and a TV newscaster. He also had a car and knew all the Washington hotspots. I found an apartment in Silver Spring, Maryland, within walking distance to the Metro train system, and chose furniture for my office, which was truly an executive model with large windows and high ceilings.

The phone started ringing off the hook with questions, questions, and more questions about issues I hadn't been briefed on. Eventually I figured out the regional directors had been advised of my oversight authority and were breaking me in for what they would be putting me through every day. But I had news for them: The only person who would set my agenda would be the director, not the regional offices. However, I didn't want to antagonize them. I was hoping for a working partnership. Knowing most of the directors helped me start out on the right foot. I set up a weekly conference call to share information, identify problems, and come up with ways to ultimately improve our delivery system of assistance to minority entrepreneurs.

What I didn't know at the time was that Bolton was getting blasted by some of the minority business organizations for his attitude. A lot of people thought he was arrogant. He was even being put down by some of his own hires. I tried to soothe some of the discontent, but most of the damage had been done before I came on board. Frankly, I was impressed with him and liked him as a person. He was sharp and methodical. Being a retired military captain, he was used to doing things a certain way. Without that kind of discipline, he tended to micromanage the agency and write off some of the bureaucrats.

And when a bunch of bureaucrats with seniority get the political players on your case, you're in trouble. Ken was in trouble.

After about eight months, rumors began to circulate that Ken's days were numbered. I started to take them seriously the day my buddy Winston asked if I was going to throw my hat in the ring for the appointment. The answer was, "No!" As associate director, I already had been given a bird's eye view of the pressure and political and impediments thrown in your way, all so the agency's enemies could prove to Congress that the program was ill-advised and doomed for failure. I had already given the best part of two decades to the program; I didn't want to end it with a heart attack.

Since I was so adamant about it, Winston said he felt comfortable in putting his name in. Then Joe Lira asked me the same question. Obviously, he, too, had his eye on the top spot.

A week later, Ken called me into the office and gave me the news about his departure. It was a sad day, but the agency had to go forward. That following Monday, I received a call from the Secretary's office. The deputy in charge of reviewing applicants and recommending the next director to Mosbacher wanted to talk to me at a given hour. I got those butterflies in my stomach again. I knew it was about the agency, but what?

But the meeting turned out to be a relaxed, informative conversation about minority programs and what they needed to continue their role at Commerce. We went back and forth before he finally asked, "Why haven't you thrown your hat into the ring?" I explained my reasons and he understood. But two days later he called again: "Would you be interested in taking the number two spot?"

"Sure. Does a raise go with it?"

I could hear him smile. "That's what I like about you. You're up front all the way."

I asked who was going to be the director.

"Joe Lira. Do you have any problems with him?"

"No, but what happened to John Winston?"

The explanation was pure Washington politics: They wanted one African American, one Latino. It didn't matter which held which position, but having both Winston and me in the number one and two spots would be one black man too many.

Within twenty-four hours, the news was out and the calls started coming from the regional directors. Yes, they heard correctly. Lira was the new director. Bailey was the deputy. All I kept hearing was, "Why didn't you go for it?"

Truth be told, all those questions did stir second thoughts. But the decision had been made and it was time to move on. Secretary Mosbacher came down the hall to congratulate us. But what about my buddy John? I assumed he would move up to my spot of associate director. But Joe had other plans. The competition for the director's slot did not sit well with him. Joe went beyond the agency to support an outside choice for the slot, Mr. Bhargava. Though he was academically qualified, he was not a mentor of minority enterprise programs. The regional directors would eat him up.

It was obvious to the senior staff that Joe wanted to get rid of John, but I told him I would not stand by and let that happen. The line had been drawn in the sand and the teams chosen: John and me on one side, Joe and the new man on the other.

As predicted, Bhargava got nowhere with the regions and he was reaching a high pitch of frustration. Joe asked me to help him with some of the tough ones: Chicago, Atlanta, and California. For the sake of the program, I agreed to help when I could.

My new responsibilities included speaking engagements. The requests came through the director's office, so he cherry-picked the bigger ones and gave me the smaller stuff. He did all the Latino groups and gave me the African Americans. At home, I had worked closely with the Hispanic community, but now I was being segregated again. Another jolt was having to have my speeches cleared, or in most cases, prepared for me. After questioning this, I was reminded that I was representing the administration, and that it was standard policy for all appointees. One of the speechwriters suggested I write my own speech, submit it for clearance, and maybe with a little massaging it would get a pass.

I never thought I would be working so many hours. A forty-hour week is only for the lower grade employees. Appointees and senior-grade administrators usually work sixty to eighty. Saturday became part of the work week, but I didn't have much else to do. I was homesick for Anna and the children and grandchild. There were weekends when I didn't have conversations with anyone for twenty-four, sometimes forty-eight hours, except for the telephone calls home. The heavy workload kept me from getting depressed. I told myself that I was on a four-year theatrical engagement and every day was another show. I was a master performer and producer for the "U.S. America Show," featuring George Bush and a cast of millions.

When I finally began to get all the responsibility under control, I let myself play tourist on some weekends and enjoy the museums, art, concerts, and historic tours Washington has to offer. I began to appreciate the solitude amid the Washington scene. Union Station became a personal favorite, with restaurants, shops, and a movie theater with the city's best popcorn, all located at a Metro stop.

It also was good to visit the minority business centers in the cities where I gave speaking engagements. But sometimes those became first-hand reminders of how people perceived the program as an unfair giveaway. In some instances, the federal agencies charged with implementing the program were the worst offenders when it came to enforcement. The challenge was to remind people that helping minority entrepreneurs helped the economy as a whole. It's called a "hand up," not a "hand out." In the past twenty years, the number of minority-owned business in the country had grown fivefold, from almost none to about a million.

It was one thing to announce the start of new programs such as Total Quality Management — a system that had been tried to great success in Japan and the private sector — but implementing them was the challenge. Remember, bureaucrats don't respond to change as quickly as the private sector. My secretary taught me how to get things through the system. "Work the system, don't fight it," was her reminder whenever I would get frustrated with how long it took to get permission for budget or policy decisions. But I learned. The bureaucrats were there when I came, and they would be there when I have gone. I had to give them credit for putting up with political appointees every four or eight years; each of them with new ideas of how they are going to make government work.

I still had the same goal as in Nevada: Help people to help themselves. I told the director, "I don't want to change the basic regional structure, I just want to make it more responsive to the needs of the clients." I wanted to look back on my time in Washington knowing I left the system in better shape than I found it.

One of the new ideas we developed was the super-center concept to put small minority-owned businesses into the mainstream, midsize business culture. We had identified some who were ready to graduate. A few good contracts with the big boys who were getting the billion-dollar contracts from the government, and they could make it work. The super centers were charged with the task of explaining their services to these big boys in hopes of developing a relationship.

Once the prototype centers were set up, it became the responsibility of the regional offices to give the needed oversight to structure a good marketing program for the various federal agencies in charge of the big procurement contracts. The Department of Defense was the major spending agency. The Gulf War, in which U.S.-led forces drove Saddam Hussein's Iraq army from Kuwait in early 1991, had created new business opportunities for the reconstruction of Kuwait. Under Mosbacher, the Department of Commerce was lining up companies with experience in international commercial contracts covering all areas of trade and construction. The press played up the size of the contracts. One day as I watched the news, I thought, 'I don't see any minorities in that trip they're taking to split up the pie.'

Bingo! The light that brings on my best ideas came on again. What a good opportunity for the super centers to get in on the Desert Storm action. In the first six months of reconstruction, a little work trickled down, but nothing outstanding. This was a little disappointing, but par for the course. It was time to do something outstanding. My show-business instincts reared their head and said, 'Let's do something dramatic and productive.' If the big boys could take a marketing trade mission to the Persian Gulf, why couldn't we do the same thing with a group of minority contractors?

THE DIRECTOR LOVED THE IDEA, ESPECIALLY when I passed on the fact that the State Department had assured me nothing like this had ever been done before with minorities. I naturally suggested he should lead the expedition, but he was very gracious and said, "Your idea, your mission. I'll do the next one, if we decide to try the same thing in Mexico."

Of course, I had no idea how much red tape was involved in putting together an official mission that fell under both the commerce and state departments. The state embassy in each country hosts your activities, and attaches from Commerce set up your business meetings.

To help with all this, I was told to get in touch with a Mr. Fred Volcansek, the deputy assistant secretary for Basic Industries in the International Trade Administration. I had never heard of him, or for that matter, a division in ITA called Basic Industries. Fred was assigned to be the mission's co-leader, and I would soon realize what a lucky choice that would be. He was thoroughly up on every step that must be taken to make this project a success.

At first, I figured we would be able to plan and develop the project in a couple of months. That was way off target. By the time Fred outlined the necessary protocol, including secret service investigation of the mission participants and arranging audiences with the Crown Prince of Kuwait and the Emir of Bahrain, I realized it would be more like six months.

We started in April 1991, with Fred tackling the travel and scheduling mechanics, and me trying to figure out who got to go. My office reached out by phone to about two hundred minority-owned companies, soliciting applications for the fifteen spots we had room for on the trip. We were flooded with applicants, but we wanted only businesses that had both the expertise and the capability to make competitive bids; those with marketing capability and a record of quality in a wide range of businesses, from the expected construction and engineering to communications, computer maintenance, and even pollution control.

By the end of November, I had narrowed down a list of potentials so strong that we were allowed to take two more company representatives, seventeen in all. On January 9' 1992, everyone assembled at the Department of Commerce for a pre-mission briefing, followed by a bus trip to the White House. Chief of Staff Samuel Skinner closed the round of briefings there, saying the President wanted Americans to realize we are all part of a global economy.

Then we were off to the airport and an eleven-day tour of five regions in the Middle East, our entourage taking up most of the business class section of the airplane. Our first stop was Riyadh, Saudi Arabia. We were greeted by a battery of Saudi officials and members of our embassy on the tarmac of the landing Strip, and escorted to a private meeting room where we were officially welcomed to Saudi Arabia.

Each of our stops included social as well as political greetings. In most cases, Fred and I handled the political and press meetings, under the careful eye of a state department representative from each respective embassy. The business coordination was done by the commercial attaches of the state department along with the Chambers of Commerce in the major economic centers we visited: Kuwait City in Kuwait; Dubai and Abu Dhabi in the United Arab Emirates; and Bahrain in Manama. (Abu Dhabi was not on the original itinerary, but they requested us after the mission was brought to their attention. We were thrilled with that, as they are one of the major banking centers in the Middle East.)

Each stop included a presentation from Fred or me and an introduction of the mission's business. The setup was that of a typical trade fair. Each business had a booth to display products and meet one-on-one with potential clients. A few times, the advance publicity attracted more people than we expected, and we stayed late to accommodate the response.

The press in each country gave our arrival strong news coverage. The English-language newspapers rarely mentioned our minority business origins, except in my title or that of our agency. Instead, they emphasized the promotion of trade between small and medium-sized firms in the respective countries. Not too many people in the Middle East even understood the phrase "minority business." To them, it was all American business. In the first meeting with some of the younger Arabs, they asked me, "Why do you keep talking about minority business? What's that? Is that a different business?"

The fact that we had racial separations in our distinctions was foreign to them. I found it difficult to explain. Fred and I agreed, "We're getting them confused. Let's just call it 'small business.'" And that's what we did for the balance of the trip. Whatever you wanted to call us, we were there to do business and not to get hung-up in social issues. It was kind of refreshing to be considered just plain Americans for a change.

The Middle East was new to most of our "rainbow coalition" that included Asian, Native American, and Iranian company heads. It might be old news to those who travel for U.S. oil companies, but it was surprising to us to stay in a Best Western hotel in Kuwait and always be surrounded by people who spoke English. Even though the Iranian merchants on our team spoke Arabic, the Kuwaitis wanted them to speak English and made that very evident. We were warned to respect local customs and not talk politics. Some of our entrepreneurs were dismayed to learn the Middle East was virtually liquor-free. Fred didn't want us to look like a bunch of drunks, but one of the lower-echelon representatives let slip to one of our exceptionally thirsty entrepreneurs that the one place you could get a drink was the U.S. Consulate. The fool got loaded, and the rest of us wondered how, so he had to spill. I don't know whatever happened to the guy at the consulate who over-served him.

The trip garnered more than $30 million in contracts and launched four international companies, matching the skills and know-how of the minority entrepreneurs with the Arab money. At least four company presidents testified enthusiastically to lawmakers. Gordon Yamada, of the Arlington, Virginia-based Executive Resource Associates, said a product called Sand Glue, which binds soil and sand particles, was so well-received that he conducted instant sales negotiations and already was booked for an immediate return to the Middle East.

I told the lawmakers that the commerce department "opened every door in support of the mission, doors that will lead — and already have — to unbelievable opportunities for qualified minority firms." I think my chest swelled a bit when I said that.

THE MIDDLE-EAST TRIP WENT OFF WITHOUT A hitch, but I wish I had Secret Service protection for one of my regional center visits to Atlanta. During the Small Business Week celebration there, I got into a very serious difference of opinion on some management issues with the regional director and pulled rank on him. The argument continued as we entered the elevator, and suddenly he punched me right in the head. I went down on one knee and almost went out; others separated us before I had the chance to throw a return punch. I sometimes wish now they hadn't stopped me, but it was better to retain my dignity and my cool, even though I was destined to have a bad headache.

Another lesson in government bureaucracy: Even with an offense this serious, it was going to take a year of grievance procedure to get this guy fired. I was overwhelmed with telephone calls and correspondence on the director's behalf; he had been in the system for twenty years or more, etc. etc. But bureaucrats have other tools, and one of them is known as a transfer. We decided to station this guy in Washington for an indefinite period of time; this would encourage either a resignation or a major life change.

A lot of us seemed destined for a move if Bush didn't win a second term against presidential challenger Bill Clinton. Just before the 1992 election, I helped my friend and early ally John Winston move over to the executive loan program at the Federal Communications Commission. After a few calls and letters on his behalf, he was set up in a job that wouldn't change with a new administration. Good thing; John moved just before Clinton won the election.

All of the presidential appointees at Commerce were handing in their resignations and saying good-bye to the career employees at MBDA. In December, Clinton's transition team started to take over and made it very clear they wanted everyone out before January 1. I had planned to be home for Christmas anyway, so I didn't mind the rush job. I had been asked to stay over for a six-month transition period. But the attitude of the new team was so imposing and hostile, I didn't think I could take the arrogance and the feeling of being treated like a loser. Besides, they were all young enough to be my children. The only attraction would be the opportunity to work with Ron Brown, the new secretary of commerce and the first African American to serve in the post. Brown was a supporter of minority enterprise and I was very impressed with him (he would die in a 1996 plane crash during a trade mission to Croatia).

But it was time to go home. I had been away from Anna and my family and friends long enough. It was a great experience and I was going to miss a lot of things: The social world, the spacious office, the limo rides to appointments. The opportunity to meet heads of state, and to be greeted by Middle Eastern royalty. I think I knew a little bit how Bush must have felt as he flew out of Washington, too.

Chapter 11

Retirement? Maybe Someday

I WAS ALMOST SIXTY-SIX WHEN I RETURNED TO Las Vegas and began to reacquaint myself with my old life and routines. But my insatiable appetite to stay busy wasn't about to let me take life easy. During my tenure in Washington, Anna had closed the Baby Grand. When our manager got sick, she had to take over the opening, closing, and inventory stocking. It all got to be more responsibility than she was up for with me out of town, and we sold the business in 1992.

I wasn't back in town a month before I was flying back to Washington to discuss a position with the National Association of Minority Business, which wanted to be the major marketing tool for midsized minority-owned enterprise. We agreed that with an assistant running the

Washington office, modern technology would allow me to stay in Las Vegas.

Everything was fine for the first six months, before complaints began piling up about my not being available to trouble-shoot all the problems with the individual companies and their contracts. These tasks were not in my agreement, but I helped where I could. My assistant was getting calls for all kinds of help and felt she was doing my job. My unplanned trips were turning the travel budget upside down. It became clearer and clearer that this wasn't a gig you could do from Las Vegas. After a year, we mutually decided I would work on a task basis when they needed me. This worked out better, and I helped market some of the companies for several years.

IT CAME TO MY ATTENTION THAT A NUMBER OF local elementary schools were not up to Nevada's academic standards. A number of these schools had mostly African American and Mexican students, who weren't getting enough parental support with homework or sometimes were just lacking someone to tell them to turn off the TV and study.

Talks with some of the teachers turned out to be a window through which I could see what kind of resources the schools would need. Of all the potential solutions, a tutorial program seemed like the one that would be most direct and effective. What if something could be set up to provide scholarship funds for schools to add more hours to their under-funded programs? But there had to be a vehicle, a legal instrument with a recognizable name. And I wanted that name to represent historical black commitment to race and country, a name that would be respected by the white community as well the black.

I suggested the name of Frederick Douglass, the abolitionist and reformer. The Frederick Douglass Educational Scholarship Fund was born in 1994. We assembled a bipartisan board of directors and adopted the regular scholarship programs for high school students. Our ongoing consultant, Frank Russell, has done an outstanding job of fundraising and program coordination for our annual gala. Now came the opportunity to present my idea of helping the elementary schools with their tutorial programs. "If we don't place proper emphasis at the elementary level, we may lose some of them forever," I said when soliciting support from the taxi companies, casinos, and minority entrepreneurs.

Over the years, it has been a challenge to keep the focus on target. The demands change with every generation, and new social frustrations of the times creep into the classrooms. We try to put our limited financial resources into student support that might not be available from other organizations that strictly finance tuition costs. The demand is greater than our supply, but we do a good job with what we generate from our annual galas.

After a couple of trips and cruise, I began to think about restricting the Nevada Institute of Business. There were still plenty of eductaional opportunities that were not being offered on an academic level in the field of finance, materials procurement, character development, and a host of environmental "Waco" subjects. For some reason I could not settle on any subject other than the Institute's main course, "Starting a Small Business." To show you how far off course I was, the study school plan that I had been doing at the Institute had been taken over in part by my daughter with a program called, "The Micro Business Program" and it was going great guns. Kim had grown up around business and has a good feel for innovative approaches to teaching. Not wanting to compete with her program, especially with hers being free, and mine having tuition charges, I figured I had better go back to my possilibities that I could pursue.

Sometimes if you don't concentrate too hard and allow your mind to free flow, it surfaces some really good ideas. Some would call this dreaming. Remember some, in fact most of the innovative changes and progress through the ages started as a dream in someone's mind. the trick is to be able to turn that dream into reality.

ONE DAY, WHILE I WAS GETTING MY DAILY DOSE of TV, my foot started into motion as I heard the rat-a-tat-tat of Florida A&M University's Marching "100" during a halftime show. My mind flashed back to Morehouse days, and how the athletics got all the glory even though our glee club was better in its respective field. How many people are aware of the great-quality choirs of the historical black colleges? What a wonderful thing it would be to bring some of these choirs to Las Vegas.

I couldn't go to sleep; this idea kept building in my brain. Why not do a national TV show directly from the stage of one of the hotels, or from the University of Nevada, Las Vegas? My turning and twisting in the bed was keeping Anna awake, so I ran the idea past her. She thought it sounded good, and would sound even better in the morning after a good night's sleep.

The idea for the Las Vegas Vocal Extravaganza in Black kept getting bigger in the daylight hours. I tapped my community relationships to put together a planning committee with a longtime friend, Marilyn Gubler. We invited the Equal Opportunity Board to be the not-for-profit sponsor. When we asked for assistance from the Las Vegas Convention and Visitors Authority, they sent us to the authority's special events committee to work up a proposal for PBS, which had mostly ignored Las Vegas because the commercial casino headliners and production shows were a bad fit with its arts-oriented programming. But black kids singing classical selections and spirituals? Right up their alley.

The convention authority wanted to make sure we would get the full support of the schools; it didn't want to see a show with its name attached go off half-cocked. I suggested we invite ten to twelve schools to Vegas for a planning session. Within ten days, all twelve target schools responded with a big thumb's up. A two-day meeting helped to iron out when to schedule the event — spring break proved to be the most agreeable answer — and how to structure the first-through-third-place cash prizes for the winners.

When you started figuring how to house, feed, and transport all those students and a technical crew, you have a lot on your hands. Artemus Ham Concert Hall on the UNLV campus emerged as the most logical base for the program. Our first show in April 1997 featured the great Ruth Brown and Joe Williams as the guest vocal stars. Johnny Pate, Joe's musical director, wrote an official theme song using my lyrics. Three of the major hotels, MGM, the Excalibur, and Circus Circus helped us with rooms and food. Dianna and Willard Booth took care of transportation. This type of partnering is what makes me love Las Vegas. The gaming community is tough in some ways and a pussycat in others. This town has a big heart when you need one. This was the same Las Vegas that I had to fight to recognize our civil rights some thirty years ago. Time does bring about change and it is gratifying when you can be a part of it.

The extravaganza continued another four years, though we changed the format from a contest to an annual "special," featuring guest stars such as Marla Gibbs, Tony Brown, Bobby Jones, Brock Peters, and Gladys Knight. Since Gladys had converted to the Mormon faith and was recording a gospel album with the Brigham Young University Choir, we invited them to perform with her on the show. Not only did the black and white student choirs blend musically, but they found a common ground of camaraderie and mutual acceptance: music. The specials showcased a period of America's history that can only be found in the choirs of the historic black colleges. They stand today as the guardians of a music that is true Americana. Negro spirituals are the very foundation of jazz, blues, and later swing. You have to salute the directors who, with slight budgets and sometimes in the face of indifference, honor the commitment to keep sacred the music that started it all. I'm proud of the five specials that gave many people an opportunity to hear, perhaps for the first time, Negro spirituals in their true form song by fourth- and fifth-generation descendants. For me, they brought back memories of going to church as a boy in Cleveland, singing in community groups or the Morehouse Glee Club, and my early days in Las Vegas at the Second Baptist Church. Kathy Kidd, my assistant producer, did a great job of coordinating these events. It took a lot of work off my back.

MY WIFE AND I WERE WAITING FOR A GATE ASsignment in the Miami airport one day, when I noticed a line of people waiting to give their bags to a uniformed young man, who then put them one at a time through a machine that literally wrapped them up in a material that was neat to the eye. I was knocked off my feet with the process. It took less than five minutes to wrap a bag and it cost $5.00 to $7.00, depending on the size. I counted six stations and they were all doing great business. I immediately saw the value of the operation and the security it offered.

During my Washington years, Anna and I attended a formal dinner party for the Chinese ambassador, welcoming him to the MBE program. Anna had carefully packed her dress, only to find it missing when our non-stop flight arrived in DC I was told this had been happening quite a bit recently, so I figured one of the skycaps must know something. I contacted the head skycap, told him I had worked on behalf of his Las Vegas counterparts to get contracts with the airlines, and asked him for some help. He told me to go back to the hotel and wait. Around midnight, I got a call from the airport: the dress had been found.

Needless to say, I was intrigued with this process that would protect your baggage contents all along the route. It was a great idea, and we needed it in Las Vegas. Horacio Lopez, my old NEDCO associate, helped track down the company, Secure Seal, and nail down the franchise rights for Las Vegas. The County Commission signed off on a lease with the airport authority without us even having to once mention our ties to the minority community.

Our initial rollout was greeted with curiosity from both the travelers and the airlines. After a couple of months, the airlines began to see how useful the wrap was for passengers carrying large stuffed animals and bags that were coming apart. But after six months, we had yet to reach a break-even point. Our salaries couldn't compete with other airport departments, which were recruiting our best people.

We made operational changes and offered tips for skycaps referrals. I spent two days at the airport, just observing and asking questions. Why was the action so much better in Miami than ours? A call to Miami finally turned up some information it would have been nice to know at the outset. Turns out that eighty to eighty-five percent of the wraps in that airport were for passengers headed to Central and South America. They come to Miami to shop for items not found in their country or only available at inflated prices. That made baggage theft very lucrative for thieves. The theft ratio in Las Vegas was minimal by comparison, and Las Vegas as a shopping destination was still in its infancy. After a year and a half, we pulled the plug on the bag-wrapping. It was a good try. I often think of how the business would have been affected by the new security measures that are in place today at the airport.

Anna and I were standing in the state capitol building in Carson City. I started thinking back to a journey there some forty years ago, as part of a group lobbying for civil rights legislation. I still remember the total indifference, and being turned away from motels and restaurants. On the long drive up there, we would stop at the Church of God in Christ to pick up box lunches. In lieu of being able to rent a room, we had to change our clothes and wash up in the restrooms in the basement of the Assembly building. We didn't get any legislation passed that time, but went through the Jim Crow treatment to let our voices be heard. We promised we would be back again.

Now, here we were in a new building and a new day in May of 1999. Anna and I were being honored as outstanding citizens of the state of Nevada for our public service. We received standing ovations as the resolutions were read in front of the Senate and Assembly. I told Anna the only other time that I felt a rush through my body like this one was when the joint session voted the passage of the equal rights legislation, a bill so many of us had worked for. Things still aren't perfect, but they are a hell of lot better than eating out of a lunch box and dressing in the restroom.

After living and working in Nevada for over fifty years and being a part of its history, I find myself looking at the young people — especially my young brothers and sisters of color — and asking, where do we go from here? We have opened the doors of opportunity. Are you ready to walk in? This question is constantly on my mind. Whenever I have the chance, I preach to our young people; I stress that education is one of the keys to true freedom. Education — and I include the trades and craft unions' apprenticeship programs within that term — offers opportunities to those who are willing to take a chance regardless of the impediments thrown in your way because of your color or gender.

I often think about that long drive from New York to Las Vegas in 1955, wondering if I was ready for a new lifestyle and trying to remember now whether I even realized what kind of adventures and opportunities awaited. To be a part of a continuing dynamic such as Las Vegas is a blessing. In its early, sparsely populated days, you could rub shoulders with the governor, mayor, and state legislators. Getting that close to those people back east was next to impossible. Though Las Vegas was a town of segregation and discrimination, the same small size and inbred political structure that fostered racism also made it a land of opportunity. And for me, that was not mere business opportunity but the chance to fight unjust policies. I am proud to contribute my son John, a brilliant attorney, and my innovative and committed daughter Kimberly, to equal justice and opportunity for all Nevadans.

As I gained community influence, I used it to encourage the political system to recognize and support the reasonable demands of minority workers such as black firefighters and police officers. When the police department denied the promotion of a black lieutenant, Larry Bolden, even though he had twice passed the exam to become a captain, the next step was court. Most of the lawyers were afraid to take his case, but in walked Harry Reid, an attorney who was respected in the Mormon community that held a lot of sway over Las Vegas. Harry (now Senate majority leader, if you didn't recognize the name) won the case and Larry Bolden became the first African American to wear double bars in Nevada history. I threw a celebration party at Sugar Hill for Larry, Harry, and the community that helped raise funds for his defense. This was just one of many times the black and white community rallied together for justice.

Sometimes a policy of denial is so ingrained that it takes drastic action to start a reversal. Affirmative action programs angered some citizens of this country, who felt it was discrimination in reverse. But really, it was a quick fix to an old problem that had not been given the attention it deserved. The programs weren't meant to stay in place forever; they were meant to summon the soul and ingenuity of this country. I was part of this movement, but in my view it's now time to move on. Out with the old, in with the new. African Americans are interwoven in the fabric of America, and I have lived to see an African American become president. We as a nation can no longer afford unproductive partisan relationships. We must utilize every talent we can muster. Will we continue to be a world leader? Yes, if we all work together. It won't be easy. But there's one thing I've said my whole life: Who said it was going to be easy?